MOTIVATION

Motivation

BRIAN TRACY

AMACOM AMERICAN MANAGEMENT ASSOCIATION
New York · Atlanta · Brussels · Chicago · Mexico City
San Francisco · Shanghai · Tokyo · Toronto · Washington, D.C.

Bulk discounts available. For details visit:
www.amacombooks.org/go/specialsales
Or contact special sales:
Phone: 800-250-5308 / E-mail: specialsls@amanet.org
View all the AMACOM titles at: www.amacombooks.org

This publication is designed to provide accurate and authoritative information in regard to the subject matter covered. It is sold with the understanding that the publisher is not engaged in rendering legal, accounting, or other professional service. If legal advice or other expert assistance is required, the services of a competent professional person should be sought.

Library of Congress Cataloging-in-Publication Data

Tracy, Brian.
Motivation / Brian Tracy.
     pages cm
Includes index.
ISBN 978-0-8144-3311-9 — ISBN 0-8144-3311-1 1. Employee motivation.
  I. Title.
HF5549.5.M63T734 2013
658.3'14—dc23

                                                              2012049357

About AMA

American Management Association (www.amanet.org) is a world leader in talent development, advancing the skills of individuals to drive business success. Our mission is to support the goals of individuals and organizations through a complete range of products and services, including classroom and virtual seminars, webcasts, webinars, podcasts, conferences, corporate and government solutions, business books, and research. AMA's approach to improving performance combines experiential learning—learning through doing—with opportunities for ongoing professional growth at every step of one's career journey.

Printing number
10 9 8 7 6 5 4 3 2 1

CONTENTS

Introduction

IN ANY ORGANIZATION, the greatest untapped resource, and the most expensive, is its people. The greatest potential for growth, productivity, performance, achievement, and profitability lies within the skills and abilities of the average person. In this book, you will learn one of the most important functions of management—the ability to motivate others to peak performance. You will learn how to use some of the very best ideas discovered in the last fifty years to enable your people to contribute their maximum to the organization.

One of the things we know is that you cannot motivate other people, but you can remove the obstacles that stop them from motivating themselves. All motivation is self-motivation. As a manager, you can create an environment where this potential for self-motivation is released naturally and spontaneously.

According to Robert Half and Associates, the average person works at about 50 percent of capability. The other 50 percent is largely wasted throughout the working day in idle conversation with coworkers, or when we waste time on the Internet, come in late, leave early, take extended coffee breaks and lunches, and handle personal business.

One of the reasons for this time wastage, which is one of the greatest financial drains on any organization, is that people are not motivated and focused enough on their work; they lack the urgency and direction to get the work done before anything else. This is a challenge that a good manager can resolve.

Tap Into the Unused 50 Percent

Your job is to tap into the unused 50 percent that the company is paying for, and to channel that time and energy into producing more and better work.

The purpose of a business is to get the highest ROE (return on equity) from the amount of capital invested in the company. The goal of management is to get the highest ROE (return on energy) from the people who work there. Financial capital is calculated in dollars. Human capital consists of the mental, emotional, and physical energies of the individual. Your job as a manager is to maximize this human capital and focus it on achieving the most valuable and important results possible for the organization.

Remove the Demotivators

There are two major demotivators in life and work. They are both factors that begin in early childhood and carry forward into adult life. They are often referred to as negative habit patterns or conditioned responses to stimuli.

The first of these demotivators is the fear of failure. This is the greatest single obstacle to success and achievement in adult life. Because of destructive criticism in childhood, adults grow up afraid of making a mistake or failing at their work. This fear serves as a form of paralysis and holds people back from taking risks, volunteering for new responsibilities, or extending themselves in any way. Fear of failure continually creates reasons or excuses for nonperformance.

The second major demotivator is the fear of rejection. This hurdle arises in early childhood when parents practice "conditional love" on their children. They make their love and support conditional upon the child performing to some undetermined high standard. The child then grows up hypersensitive to the opinions, comments, and feedback of others, especially the boss in the workplace.

This fear of rejection is also a fear of criticism, condemnation, or censure—the fear of making a mistake and being dumped on for it. Excellent managers are those who practice "unconditional acceptance" with each employee, causing all employees to feel safe and secure with their boss and in their work.

Drive Out Fear

There are many other reasons for demotivation and poor performance, but these are the two main fears that prevent people from extending themselves to do their very best. Successful organizations and managers are those that consciously and deliberately remove these barriers. They make it all right to fail or to make mistakes. They make it clear that nobody gets rejected, dumped on, criticized, or threatened with retaliation for making a mistake. The best managers create an environment where people feel free to be the best they can be.

W. Edwards Deming, the father of total quality management, said that one of his fourteen keys to building a high-performance organization was to "drive out fear." In the absence of fear, people tend to perform and produce at a higher level than ever before.

In this book, you will learn a series of practical, proven methods and techniques that you can use to reduce the fears of failure and rejection, increase the propensity to try more things, and cause people to feel terrific about themselves when they work for you. Only when people feel good about themselves are they motivated to work hard and succeed.

Each of these ideas is based on years of research and practice. Sometimes implementing just one of these ideas can transform an average work environment into a superior work environment almost overnight.

The Key Factor

The key factor in motivation and in peak performance is just one thing: the nexus between the manager and the managed. It is what takes place at the moment of contact or communication between the manager and the employee that is the key determinant of performance, effectiveness, productivity, output, and profitability of an organization. The point at which the two people connect, whether positively or negatively, is where the past, present, and future performance of the individual and the organization is determined.

When this contact between the boss and the subordinate is positive and supportive, then performance, productivity, and output of the individual will reach its highest level. If this point of contact between the manager and the managed is negative for any reason at all, performance and output will decline. A negative relationship with the boss will trigger fears of failure, rejection, and disapproval.

The ideas in this book are all focused on improving the quality of this nexus or meeting point between the manager and the staff. Everything you do to improve this intersection or contact improves the overall quality of your work life, no matter where you are on the ladder of management.

One last point before we begin: As Einstein said, "Nothing happens until something moves." By the same token, nothing happens until someone moves. None of these ideas will be of any value until and unless you take action on them—preferably as soon as possible.

Effective managers are intensely action-oriented. When they hear a good idea, they move quickly to implement the idea and put it into action. Therefore, as you read this book, if you learn anything that you think can help you to motivate your staff to a higher level, don't delay. Practice it immediately, that very day. You will be amazed at the results.

ONE

The X Factor

THERE WERE several studies done by management consultants in Europe in the late 1940s and early 1950s comparing the output of British automobile manufacturing plants to those of West German plants. What they found was that the most efficient German auto manufacturing plants were outproducing the British plants by as much as four to one. At first, the British researchers blamed the disparity on the fact that the German plants were all new, having been rebuilt after World War II, while most of the British plants were old and still using machinery from the 1930s.

To test this theory, they compared new British plants to new German plants that were each manufacturing the same size of car, each with a unionized workforce, and each using the same technology and materials. They found that between the best-managed and worst-managed plants in both countries, there was still a production difference of four to one.

This productivity difference, which could not be explained by material or technical factors, became known as the "X factor." The discovery of the X factor, now called the psychological factor, led to a revolution in management that has taken place in the last sixty years throughout the free world.

Up until the Great Depression of the 1930s, almost all advances in management were a result of advances in technology, science, and production processes. Since World War II, most of the great advances have been managerial and psychological in nature. The X factor explains more than anything else why some companies succeed and others fail, why the top 20 percent of companies in every industry earn 80 percent of the profits, and why the most talented people are drawn to the best companies.

By tapping into the psychological factors that determine performance and productivity, you can make a dramatic difference in your effectiveness as a manager and in your ability to get results.

The Command Center

The psychological factor really comes down to a very simple point: the self-concept. The discovery of the self-concept is perhaps the most important breakthrough in the development of human potential in the twentieth and twenty-first centuries.

The self-concept is the belief structure or value system of the individual. It forms and develops from early childhood and is a composite of all of the emotions, experiences, decisions, education, and events of a person's life up to the present day. The self-concept determines how a person thinks about himself, feels about himself, and sees himself relative to the rest of the world.

The self-concept is like the command center that sits at the core of personality and productivity. It is what governs individual performance, behavior, and output. All changes or improvements in external performance and behavior begin with improvements in the self-concept; to put it another way, all changes in the *outer* world of the individual begin with changes in the *inner* world.

The Self-Concept and Performance

The self-concept is made up of three components: the self-ideal, the self-image, and the self-esteem. Let's take each of these in order.

The individual's *self-ideal* is a summary picture of what the person aspires to be in life. It is made up of the goals, dreams, hopes, and ideals that the person has about himself and what is possible for him to become at some time in the future.

In the world of work, the individual's self-ideal is influenced by corporate values, the role models represented by the senior people in the organization, and the corporate culture surrounding employees.

The second part of the self-concept is the *self-image*. This is the way a person thinks she is viewed by others. People who see themselves as likable, confident, and competent will tend to do a much better job than people who see themselves as not particularly good at their work.

Your self-image is greatly influenced by the way people treat you daily. When people are treated as though they are valuable, important, and respected, they see themselves and think about themselves in a more positive way. As a result, they perform at higher levels and do better work.

The third part, and the core of the self-concept, is the individual's level of *self-esteem*. Self-esteem can be defined as "how much you like yourself." The more people like and respect themselves on the inside, the better they perform on the outside: They set bigger goals for themselves and higher standards for the quality of their work; when people like themselves, they also like other people more and become excellent team players.

The self-esteem is the "reactor core" of the human personality and largely determines the individual's level of energy, enthusiasm, vitality, and self-confidence.

The key to creating a peak performance organization is to create an environment of high self-esteem by removing the fears of failure and rejection that inhibit personal performance. The manager who creates a positive, high-self-esteem workplace will have higher performance, lower absenteeism, lower employee turnover, higher productivity, and fewer mistakes.

The Role of the Manager

There are seven ways that the manager can build and reinforce a positive self-concept in each employee. These practices align with seven motivators:

1. *Challenge.* Give people jobs that make them *stretch.* The more challenge that people experience in their work, the more engaged they will be and the more positive they will feel about themselves.

2. *Freedom.* Give people sufficient autonomy to work without close supervision. The more freedom that they have to get the job done on their own, in their own way, the better they feel about themselves.

3. *Control.* Set regular times for review, feedback, and discussion of the work. The more regular feedback that employees get on their performance, the better they feel about themselves and the more valuable they consider their work to be.

4. *Respect.* When you ask for people's opinions, and listen closely to them when they want to talk, they feel more valuable and important. By listening attentively and carefully considering the opinions of others—even if you, as manager, do not act on their input—you demonstrate that you respect the uniqueness of each person.

5. *Warmth.* The more your people see that you like and care about them as individuals, in addition to members of the staff, the better they will perform. By treating your people as though they are your friends and natural extensions of your corporate "family," you make them feel safer, more secure, and more important.

6. *Success Experiences.* A key to self-esteem and self-concept building is to give people jobs that they can perform successfully at their levels of experience and skill. When they complete a task, recognize and acknowledge that achievement, both privately and publicly, so that people feel like "winners."

7. *Positive Expectations.* This is perhaps the most powerful motivator of all. Nothing boosts self-esteem and improves performance more than when people sense that their boss believes that they are good and competent and that they have the ability to do the job well.

Successful companies are those that create an environment where people feel terrific about themselves. Understanding the role of the self-concept in behavior is the starting point of effectiveness in management and motivation.

ACTION EXERCISES

1. Make it a habit to treat your individual staff members as though they are valuable, important, intelligent, and competent. Look for every opportunity to build their self-esteem and self-confidence in every interaction with them.

2. Tell your staff members continually how good they are, and how impressed you are with the quality of their work. When you confidently expect people to perform at high levels, they will seldom disappoint you.

TWO

Select the Right People

SELECTING THE RIGHT people is the starting point of excellence in management. Probably 95 percent of your success as a manager resides in your ability to select the right people in the first place. If you hire the wrong people, then no matter what you do, what techniques you use, or what efforts you put in, it is not going to make very much difference. Almost all of your problems as a manager come from either selecting the wrong people or inheriting the wrong people in your position.

In his book, *Good to Great*, Jim Collins suggests that, essentially, the first job of management is to "get the right people on the bus, get the right people into the right seats on the bus, and then get the wrong people off the bus."

When Lee Iacocca was brought in to save Chrysler Corporation, it was on the verge of bankruptcy. After securing a $350 million loan guarantee to keep Chrysler operational until he could turn it around, Iacocca went methodically through the senior management of Chrysler, replacing thirty-five out of thirty-six vice presidents over a three-year period. By the time he was finished, he had completely restaffed the upper ranks of Chrysler Corporation with highly skilled and experienced car executives from all over America and around the world.

With the right people in the right places, Chrysler underwent a remarkable turnaround, transforming losses into profits. In less than three years, Iacocca completely repaid the $350 million loan guarantee and put Chrysler Corporation back into the black.

Think Through the Job

Hiring the right people in the first place is the key to managerial success. Begin by thinking through the job carefully, preferably on paper. Write out a list of all of the characteristics and qualities that you would want in the ideal person for a particular job. First, focus on the specific, measurable results and outcomes that you expect the new employee to achieve.

The second factor you look for is the set of basic skills that the person will have to have to get the results that the job requires. Interview carefully to make sure that the candidate has demonstrated in the past the skills you've identified for the job. As Peter Drucker said, "Only past performance is an accurate predictor of future performance."

Finally, hire as much for attitude, personality, and character as you do for job skills. Make sure that the new person will fit in comfortably with your company culture and work well with yourself and others. If you select people with the right attitude and personality, you can train and manage them to do the job well.

The Law of Three

With the Law of Three, you can increase your ability to make good hires. In fact, your success rate can be as high as 90 percent, based on my experience with thousands of executives and business owners. Here is how it works, in six steps.

First, interview at least three candidates for a job. This practice forces you to slow down and compare and contrast the qualities and characteristics of different people. Second, interview the candidate that you like three different times. Remember, a job candidate will look the very best on the first interview. After that, there is a gradual deterioration as the screens fall away and the true person is revealed.

Third, interview the person you like in three different places. For some reason, many people have what I call a "chameleon complex." They appear a certain way in your office in the first interview and then seem to act and react differently when you move them into different environments.

Fourth, have any candidate that impresses you interviewed by at least three other people on your team. In too many cases, a candidate that I considered to be ideal was roundly rejected by my team and, as it turned out, for good reason.

Check References Carefully

Fifth, check at least three references from the candidate. Because of the fear of lawsuits, most employers will only give you the dates of employment of the candidate. But there are still questions that you can ask to glean useful information. When you call, say something like, "We are interviewing this person for this particular job, doing these particular activities, and having these particular responsibilities." You can then ask specific questions such as:

1. Could you tell me some of the strengths or weaknesses that this candidate would have in performing a job like this?

2. Is there anything you could tell me that would help me to make a better hiring decision?

3. Would you hire this person back again if he applied to you for a job?

If the reference is reluctant to comment on the candidate or won't answer questions 1 and 2, always ask question 3, which is the key question. If the answer is not an unequivocal "yes," you should be very cautious about hiring the candidate in the first place.

The sixth and final piece of advice is to check references three deep. That is, ask the given reference for the names of other people the candidate has worked with, so you can talk to those people, too. When you interview three additional people whose names do not appear on the candidate's resume, you may be surprised at what you learn.

Many executives have told me that this Law of Three has significantly improved the quality of the people they have hired and the effectiveness of the entire team.

The SWAN Formula

The SWAN formula was recommended some years ago by an executive recruiter named John Swan. It is a good acronym that you can use to improve your selection process. It has four letters: S, W, A, N.

S stands for smart. Hire smart people. How do you tell the intelligence of a candidate? The answer is simple. Questions! Intelligent people tend to be more curious than average people.

The *W* in the formula stands for "work hard." Look for people who are willing to work hard and who have backgrounds that indicate that they have worked long, hard hours—including evenings and weekends—at previous jobs.

The *A* stands for ambition. The proper candidate is someone who wants to move ahead in life. Ambitious people are willing and eager to take additional training; they are already reading and studying and seeking opportunities to grow, both personally and professionally.

Finally, *N* stands for people who are "nice." The likability of the candidate is a critical factor, and this quality is especially important for people who have to deal with the public or with customers of any kind. As Leona Helmsley once said in her advertisement for her hotel chain, "We don't hire people and train them to be nice; we just hire nice people."

In the final analysis, your ability to pick the right people for your team is the key to motivation. You cannot hire the wrong people and then expect to motivate them to be excellent performers for your team. It is much better that you proceed carefully and painstakingly and hire the right people in the first place.

ACTION EXERCISES

1. Identify the qualities of the best people on your team today. What can you do to be sure to hire more of them in the future?

2. The next time you hire someone, practice the Law of Three exactly as it is described in this chapter. After you have done it once from beginning to end, you will use this technique repeatedly in the future.

THREE

Start Them Strong

IN A THIRTY-YEAR research project, accounting firm Deloitte & Touche studied thousands of its employees, starting with the initial hiring process and then following employees' track records through the years in an attempt to determine the factors that would most predict high performance in the long term. What the researchers found was quite interesting.

First, they discovered that *self-selection* was a vital factor in predicting subsequent performance. The term "self-selection" refers to employees who had more than one choice of an employer. After interviewing with other companies, these employees, who were obviously talented since they were in consideration for a job at such a prestigious firm, came back to Deloitte & Touche and said very emphatically, "I want to work *here*."

In other words, they had decided for themselves that Deloitte was the best company that they could work for, and they were determined to get that particular job. Even many years later, the self-selected employees were still doing a better job and performing at a higher level than people who were less enthusiastic at the beginning.

Load Them with Work

The second factor they discovered, and the focus of this chapter, was that the managers of high performers started them off strong with lots of work, even an overload, from the very first day of employment.

Chapter One talked about the self-concept and its central role in determining the personality and behavior of the adult. Just as the self-concept of individuals forms from early childhood experience, the self-concept of employees with regard to their performance and behavior on the job begins to form from their first contact with the company. New employees are going to be influenced by their first impressions. And when their first experience or impression of the job is suddenly being up to their neck with roles, goals, and responsibilities, they quickly develop the belief that this is a place where you work hard from dawn to dusk.

It seems that for the rest of their careers with their company, employees who were given lots of work from the first day were harder workers and more focused on contribution and performance than people who were started off gradually. Conversely, the Deloitte & Touche researchers found that employees who were given lots of time to meet their cowork-ers and allowed to gradually start working at their job were, even ten years later, working at a slower pace and making a less valuable contribution.

As it happens, the number one motivator in the world of work, and the primary desire of each employee, is that the job be *challenging*. Employees want to be stretched and even to race to keep up with the work and get the job done. Interestingly enough, people may complain about being "overworked," but when pressed, they will admit they would much rather be busy than bored.

Start new employees off strong. Plunge them in over their heads by burying them in work from the first day. Give them more work than they can possibly handle, and keep adding new jobs to their list of responsibilities. When you start people off with a list of tasks and responsibilities and regularly express your confidence in their abilities to do the jobs assigned, they will rise to the challenge and become your very best performers, almost from day one.

And in addition to making the work challenging, make the work *interesting*. Nothing makes employees happier than to be loaded up with interesting work, as they start a job full of eagerness and openness to new ideas and experiences.

Practice Hands-On Management

As important as overloading them with work, you must give new employees hands-on training and support from the first day. New employees have what is called "low task-relevant maturity." This means that no matter how much work experience the employee had in the past, the meter is set back to zero at the new job: The new employee simply has no exact idea of what to do or how to do it.

For this reason, you should take new employees under your wing and give them careful step-by-step direction and guidance in doing all parts of the new job. The idea of "sink or swim" has been relegated to the history books of business. It is not a valid or intelligent way of starting a new person, if it ever was.

If you do not have the time yourself, assign your new employees to another person who will be responsible for making sure that they are thoroughly versed in the way the company works and, especially, what the job entails and how it should be done. This "buddy system" is the best way to ensure that new employees begin with a sense of confidence and belonging.

Lay a Solid Foundation

When people start off slowly at a new job, they quickly come to believe that this pace is both accepted and acceptable in the company. It is difficult later to try to get them motivated to perform at higher levels. The die is cast. The foundation is set. It is quite likely that the employee will still be performing at a lower level of activity months and years into the future.

Remember, the second letter in the SWAN formula (from Chapter Two) is "work hard." Do everything you can to make sure that people are working hard from the time they arrive until the time they depart; this way you will be creating the type of employees that are most amenable to your efforts to motivate them to ever-higher levels of performance in the future.

ACTION EXERCISES

1. When you interview prospective employees, watch for and wait for them to express an intense desire to work with you and for the company. Never hire anyone that you have to coax or talk into taking the job.

2. From now on, whenever you hire new employees, be sure that you start them off with a list of jobs to be done from the very first day. Be sure, also, to take new people under your wing to teach them the job and help them to become established as hardworking and valuable members of the team. If you, as manager, don't have time to provide this hands-on training and support, be sure to assign it to someone else.

FOUR

Communicate Clear Expectations

THE KEY TO motivation is to make people feel terrific about themselves. One way you make people feel terrific about themselves is to make them feel like winners. Everyone wants to enjoy the "winning feeling." They want to feel competent, successful, and respected by others.

In a race or competition of some kind, how do people win? Simple: They cross the finish line first.

In the world of work, how does a person win? Answer: They complete a clear, specific task. One of the great rules of work is that task completion is a source of energy, enthusiasm, and positive self-esteem.

In a survey asking employees to describe the best job they ever had, one of the most common answers was, "I always knew exactly what I was expected to do."

When asked about the worst jobs they ever had, they often said, "I never really knew what my boss expected me to do."

Whenever you communicate clear expectations, you make it possible for people to complete a clear, specific task and to feel like winners. When you communicate vague or fuzzy expectations, or no expectations at all, you deprive your staff of the ability to experience that "winning feeling."

Five Factors for Winning

To cross the finish line and feel like a winner at work, a person needs five things:

1. Clear goals and objectives, which are discussed and agreed upon.

2. Clear measurements, metrics, and standards so that the employee knows that success will be measured and determined.

3. Clear deadlines and sub-deadlines, so the employee knows exactly when the job is supposed to be completed.

4. Success experiences—that is, the employee must actually complete the job on time, on budget, and to the agreed-on standards of quality.

5. Recognition and rewards—the employee must receive acknowledgment for successful task completion by the boss, very much like the crowd cheering for a winning athlete. In addition, whenever possible, there should be both tangible and

intangible rewards that accompany the successful completion of a task.

You may have heard it said that "you can't hit a target that you can't see." For your people to feel like winners, they must have clear targets to aim for. The clearer the goals and objectives, the easier it is for people to achieve them. The more they achieve their goals, the more they feel like winners. And the more they feel like winners, the higher their self-esteem and their happiness about their work.

Many managers, including myself, have made the mistake of assigning tasks quickly because of time pressures, taking no time to discuss the job and to make sure that the employee knows exactly what is expected of him. Later, when the job is either not done, done poorly, or done differently from what you wanted, your natural tendency is to blame the employee for incompetence. But it is almost always the manager who is at fault.

Define Excellent Performance

People need to know what constitutes excellent performance of a particular job. Before you approach the employee, ask yourself, "If this job were done excellently, what would the result look like? How would I describe an excellent job?"

When you assign a job, tell the person that if this job were done excellently, it would be done by a specific time, and it would achieve a certain level of quality.

Then, be sure to inspect what you expect. The more important the job assignment, the more important it is that you monitor and check on the progress of the job on a regular basis, even daily.

People know that the task is important when you set up a regular schedule for monitoring progress, rather than if you simply assign it and appear to forget about it. Your regular checking in to see how the job is going is a way of continually affirming both the importance of the job and the importance of the person doing the job. Regular inspection of a task actually builds a sense of personal value and higher self-esteem in the person doing the job.

One of your most important responsibilities as a manager is to be sure that everyone who reports to you knows exactly what they are expected to do and in what order of importance, what constitutes successful completion of the task, and the exact deadlines for completion. When you provide your people with these ingredients, you give them the raw material that they need to perform and feel like winners.

Defining expectations is something that only you can do. If you do not define what a job done excellently is, and if you don't do it well and regularly, you deprive your staff of the "joy of work." Lack of clarity about what has to be done, and by when, is a major reason for time wastage at work and a general lack of satisfaction with the job itself.

ACTION EXERCISES

1. The next time you assign a task, take a few minutes to discuss with the employee exactly what is to be done, how it will be measured, and the deadline, and be sure the employee agrees with the task goals and objectives.

2. Once you have discussed and agreed upon a task, have the employee feed it back to you, in his own words, to ensure that what you said and what the employee heard were identical. You may at first be surprised at the misunderstandings that take place in even the simplest job assignments.

FIVE

Practice Participative Management

PARTICIPATIVE MANAGEMENT is a powerful tool for building involvement, commitment, loyalty, and ownership of the task. Employees' commitment to quality work will be in direct proportion to their involvement in setting goals and standards in the first place.

Socrates once said, "We only learn something by dialoguing about it." There is a direct one-to-one relationship between discussion and motivation. If you want your people to be motivated to do excellent work, and to enjoy high levels of self-esteem and self-confidence, they need an opportunity to discuss what they are doing with their boss on a regular basis.

For participative management to work its magic, there has to be a genuine commitment on the part of management to this process. You need to believe that it is important for people to be involved. You must feel that members of your staff are entitled to participate in determining the work they do, the standards that are set, and how they go about accomplishing the task.

Two Predictors of High Performance

Psychologists have found that the two most important predictors of high achievement in adulthood are positive expectations on the part of the parents combined with a democratic family environment.

Since adults are just children with better excuses, as we say, the same two qualities that predict high-achieving young people are the same two qualities that determine a high-performance work environment: positive expectations and a democratic environment.

The most effective work teams are democratic, in which the boss and the employees work together as a team, everyone fully participating and discussing what needs to be done.

The more often you meet with your staff members, the greater their sense of participation and the higher their self-esteem. One of the best analogies to use again is that of the family. Regular communications for families means getting together around the dinnertable and, with give-and-take, playing and talking. If you don't spend regular time with your family members at dinnertime, and don't communicate regularly with them when you're not together, your family life will quickly begin to deteriorate. It is the same with your work life.

Five Keys to Team Building

There are five essential elements for building a high-performance work team:

1. *Shared Goals and Objectives.* The team meets regularly to discuss the goals and objectives of the team, what needs to be done, by what time, and by which standards of quality.

2. *Shared Values and Guiding Principles.* The members of the team discuss and agree on how they are going to work together and what their common values will be, such as punctuality, accepting responsibility, helpfulness, cooperation, and keeping their promises to each other.

3. *Shared Plans of Action.* Everyone knows exactly what each member of the team is expected to do and contribute in the achievement of the larger job, and all team members commit to doing their part of the work on time and to the required standards.

4. *An Action Leader.* The manager or team leader sees her job as making sure that everyone else has whatever they need to do their jobs completely and well. The manager's job is to remove any blocks or obstacles from the path of the team members in getting their jobs done on time.

5. *Regular Review and Feedback.* The team meets on a regular basis to ask, "How are we doing?" There is positive interaction and open discussion focused

on improving the ability of the team to get more and better results.

In participative management, the manager serves as a coach or partner in the work. The job of the manager is to tell people how they are doing and to give guidance and encouragement. At participative management meetings, the manager hands out assignments, discusses work in progress, and makes sure that each person hears what the others are doing. The staff discusses everything.

People only become involved and excited about any task to the degree to which they can contribute their opinions and ideas on a regular basis. The more discussion you have about the work, what needs to be done, and the best way to accomplish it, the more commitment, loyalty and enthusiasm you generate in each person.

Keep People Informed

In surveys and assessments that are updated annually at GreatPlacetoWork.com, one of the most powerful of all motivators is feeling "in the know." Happy employees report that they felt they were fully informed about their work and everything that was going on around them. They felt like respected members of a larger entity, participating in achieving the goals and objectives of the entire company.

One of the ways that management consultants measure the climate of a company or a department is by noting the types of pronouns that employees use to describe themselves, their work, and the organization.

In the best organizations, they hear the words "me and mine" when people describe their job, and the pronouns "us and our" when describing the business. In less effective organizations, employees use the words "they, them, and the company" in referring to the organization, as though it was separate and apart from the individual employee.

One of the most important factors in highly motivated people is a sense of "ownership." Initially, the company and the manager have ownership and responsibility for setting objectives and completing tasks; as far as employees are concerned, they are merely participants in helping you, the boss, complete the task.

Instill Ownership

However, the more you participate with employees—discussing the job that needs to be done and the best way to do it—the more employees take ownership of the job, eventually seeing the job as belonging to them personally. When this "transfer of ownership" takes place, employees are much more motivated and determined to do the job well and on time, because the job is now a natural extension of themselves. It belongs to them. It is their property. It is a reflection of their personal abilities whether the job is done well.

When employees complete a job that they own personally, they get more satisfaction. They feel like winners. Their self-esteem goes up, and they are even more eager to take on additional tasks and responsibilities from which they can generate the same positive feelings.

This feeling of ownership on the part of each person who reports to you is absolutely essential in building a high-performance workplace.

ACTION EXERCISES

1. Take the time to actively engage employees in their work by sharing, discussing, and encouraging each employee to participate with you in determining the best way to perform the task or to achieve the goal.

2. Seek every way to have employees accept personal ownership of the job by asking questions, encouraging them, and listening to them when they want to talk. The more they can discuss the work with you, the more committed they will be to doing the job and doing it well.

SIX

The Four Factors of Motivation

THERE ARE FOUR factors that, together with the three R we'll discuss in the next chapter, exist in every organization and determine the levels of motivation of the staff whether positive or negative. Fortunately, each of these ingredients can be changed in a positive way—usually when a new leader replaces a leader whose management style has not been conducive to bringing out the very best in each person.

Basics of Motivation

Let's begin with the four factors that are the basics of motivating anyone, in any organization. These four factors are: 1) leadership style, 2) the reward system, 3) the organizational climate, and 4) the structure of the work.

LEADERSHIP STYLE

This is a key factor in determining how people feel about the company and how motivated they are. Very often, just changing the leader changes the psychological climate of the company and, in turn, the whole performance of people in the organization.

The appropriate leadership style depends on the goals and objectives of the organization, the people within the company, and the external environment.

In a SWAT team or a fire department, the appropriate style would be more directed and dictatorial, with the person in charge telling people what to do quickly with little concern for personal sensitivities. This style can also be found among entrepreneurial organizations, many of which are struggling for their very survival. In most cases, however, traditional top-down leadership style is no longer acceptable to today's breed of employees, who expect to be able to speak out, be heard, and have a clear influence on how they do the work.

Different Strokes for Different Folks. A second leadership style is collegial, where one person may be in charge of a department but functions at the same level and with the same knowledge and skill as his coworkers. In this type of organization, people are respected for their knowledge, skill, and ability to do the job.

Other leadership styles that have been identified are *telling, selling, persuading,* and *participating.* Each of these styles is appropriate depending on whether the employee is new or experienced, and whether there is ample time or urgency in completing the task. Sometimes, the manager is required to use different leadership styles for different people under differing circumstances.

THE REWARD SYSTEM

Every organization is characterized by a particular type of reward structure, often differing from person to person and from department to department.

As author Michael LeBoeuf says in his book, *The Greatest Management Principle in the World*: "What gets rewarded gets done." If you want more of something in an organization, simply create greater rewards for that behavior. If you want less of an activity in an organization, simply reduce the rewards, or increase the punishment or disapproval for that behavior. People respond to incentives.

It is quite common for companies to identify their most profitable products and services, and then increase the percentage of commission that salespeople will receive for selling those specific products and services, while maintaining lower commissions for less profitable items. Salespeople and managers for that matter, respond very quickly to increased or decreased financial rewards for specific behaviors or for achieving specific goals.

ORGANIZATIONAL CLIMATE

Is your company a "great place to work"? The organizational climate is deliberately created and maintained by management. It largely consists of the way that people treat each other up and down the line.

When Thomas J. Watson Sr. started IBM, he laid out the three core values of the company. These values—excellent products and services, excellent customer service, and respect for the individual—would determine the future of IBM, eventually making it the biggest and most respected computer company in the world.

The principle of "respect for the individual" was adamantly enforced at every level of the organization, both nationally and internationally. You could make almost any mistake at all at IBM, except one. You could not disrespect, demean, or insult another person, either inside or outside of the organization. Treating people badly, especially people under your authority, was grounds for dismissal, no matter how long you had been with the company.

As a result of this element of organizational climate, not only did people compete vigorously to get into IBM in the first place, but once there they were some of the happiest, most productive, and creative people in any company in any industry.

THE STRUCTURE OF THE WORK

Some work is inherently motivational, requiring creativity, imagination, and high levels of energy. Work that involves communicating, negotiating, and interacting with other people in order to gain their cooperation to get the job done quickly and well brings out the best energies of the individual. It is exciting and challenging. It is usually highly rewarding as well.

However, an enormous amount of work must be standardized, routinized, and made relatively unexciting in order to be done efficiently and cost effectively. It is hard to motivate factory workers who work on a production line all day and whose activities are carefully monitored and regulated to ensure maximum levels of productivity.

Good organizations are always trying to structure the work so as to match the nature of the work with the nature of the employee, and to make the work as interesting and enjoyable as possible.

The Leader Can Make an Immediate Difference

The reward structure, the organizational climate, and the structure of the work can be changed, but usually slowly; everything must be thought through carefully and in detail. The leadership style of an organization, however, is the one factor that can be changed quickly, and this change can make a major difference almost overnight.

There is a story of a factory whose managers were highly political and much more concerned with their own rewards and privileges than they were with the morale of the workers. The factory was demoralized, suffering low levels of productivity and high levels of defects, and it was on the verge of being shut down by the head office.

Instead of shutting the factory down, the head office sent in a new general manager, replacing the existing management completely. On his first day on the job, the general manager was waiting when the first shift of workers arrived that morning, parking their cars out in the unpaved parking lot and walking through the mud to the factory entrance.

When the entire shift had gathered, the new manager introduced himself, then in front of everybody, walked over to the reserved parking spaces lined up next to the main entrance, where the executives were accustomed to parking when they arrived at work. An assistant gave him a bucket of paint, and the new manager walked along the wall, painting out the names of the executives for whom the parking spaces had been reserved. "From now on, whoever gets here first gets the best parking space," he told the workers.

Within six months, that factory was producing at the highest level in its history, and it was one of the most productive and profitable factory operations in the entire national organization. One highly motivational leader with a clear, exciting vision for the organization can become a motivational force for change and transformation, even when everything else is unchanged.

ACTION EXERCISES

1. Review the organizational climate in your organization: Is the value of respect for the individual consistently reinforced? Communicate directly with your staff members or ask your managers to communicate to their subordinates the organization's no-tolerance policy on disrespecting any employee in any way.

2. Talk to your employees about whether they find their jobs challenging and interesting. Ask them for ideas on how they can make their jobs less routine and more exciting.

SEVEN

The Three Rs

AS WITH THE four factors of motivation (described in the previous chapter), the three Rs of motivation are found in every organization and business, and they have a major impact on employee enthusiasm and commitment. The three Rs of motivation are rewards, recognition, and reinforcement.

Rewards

Since rewards motivate and incentivize people, they must be based on performance. Specifically, they must be based on the successful completion of activities that help the organization and drive it forward toward the achievement of its goals of productivity and profitability.

Nothing else should be rewarded—not seniority, not education, not political connections. Only performance.

The only way for a reward structure to work in helping the company to be successful is when rewards are directly tied to performance that helps the overall organization.

Fast-growing organizations tend to be performance-based. The only way to get ahead in these organizations is by doing an excellent job, getting along well with all of your coworkers, and helping the company continue to grow.

In some organizations, the key to success is "how you play the game." People are paid more and promoted based on their ability to influence and manipulate other people in their climb to the top. In these organizations, the focus strays away from performance and into political activity.

Politically oriented organizations tend to be those companies that have reached a position of market dominance, where they have been profitable for a substantial period of time. Performance is no longer a primary consideration; politics is everything. These organizations almost invariably fail in competition with performance-based organizations.

TWO TYPES OF REWARDS

There are two types of rewards—tangible and intangible. Tangible rewards are money, vacations, and material objects.

The best way to use money as a reward is to give a specific amount as a bonus directly related to the performance of a task or the achievement of a goal. Some companies make the mistake of giving a person a permanent pay increase for achieving a specific performance target, but then they are locked into that higher level of pay whether or not the employee ever repeats that performance. Specific, discrete bonuses are usually better.

Intangible rewards can be things such as prizes, plaques, and awards given at annual celebrations for exceptional performance. They can be in the form of additional education, which benefits both the employee and the company, or time off from work, provided it's during periods that won't detract from employee productivity and performance and cost the company any significant money.

Public praise and commendation, especially in front of others, is a wonderful intangible reward that boosts morale and motivation and improves performance continuously over the long term. It is an "emotional" reward that has little dollar cost, yet yields big benefits.

Recognition

Managers owe their people recognition when they do a good job. One of the greatest motivations in the world of work is being recognized for having gone the extra mile and done an excellent job. On the other hand, one of the greatest complaints in the world of work is when people work very hard to do an excellent job and are then ignored by the boss for their accomplishments.

Whenever a person does anything that is exceptional, that is above and beyond the requirements of the job (or even makes a good try), the manager should give that employee recognition, both in private and in public. The rule is that whatever gets recognized gets repeated.

Reinforcement

This is one of the most powerful motivational techniques of all. Whatever you praise, approve, recognize, and reinforce is going to be repeated, and often over and over again. When you reinforce behavior by telling people how much you appreciate what they have done, it makes people feel terrific about themselves; as a result, they will continually seek new opportunities to repeat that same behavior so as to stimulate reinforcement. If you don't praise and reinforce good work and positive behaviors, you are probably going to get less effort from employees.

Many managers have the idea that a paycheck is sufficient reward for doing a good job. But that is not the way the average person sees it. Whenever employees go out of their way to do the job in an excellent fashion, they believe that recognition and reinforcement is a reward that they have justly earned.

PUSHING EMPLOYEES TO DOUBLE WOW!

One of my client companies developed four levels of performance that determined not only pay and promotion, but also bonuses at the end of the year. As I recommended previously, bonuses are the best way to use monetary rewards for performance. The four levels of performance in this company were average performance, excellent performance, wow!, and double wow!

"Average" performance meant that a person's job was in jeopardy at the end of the year. "Excellent" performance was considered the minimum standard to keep your job and to be considered for promotion.

When employees exceeded their performance requirements and did what was seen by everyone to be an especially outstanding job, they reached the third level of performance, called "wow!"

The highest performance of all was called "double wow!" Because this was an entrepreneurial organization, there were opportunities for top performers to dramatically impact the bottom line in different areas. When a person's performance was completely outside of anything that could have been expected, they received a Double Wow Award.

Excellent performers received 10 percent to 20 percent of their annual salary as a year-end bonus. Wow! performers received as much as 50 percent of their salary. Double wow! performers received bonuses that were 50 percent to 100 percent of their annual salary.

Through rewards and recognition, this company encouraged and motivated its employees to achieve exceptional performance. As a result, it was consistently rated as one of the fastest-growing and most profitable companies in its industry.

The three Rs can help you define the standard of performance in your organization. Remember that managers and organizations are going to get more of whatever they are rewarding. This means that you can quickly shape, guide, and channel the behavior and performance of your staff based on what you are consistently rewarding, recognizing, and reinforcing.

ACTION EXERCISES

1. Think of specific ways that you can reward, recognize, and reinforce the kind of behaviors and performance that you desire from your employees. Look for ways to do one or more of these things each day.

2. Ask your staff members, one at a time or as a group, what they would value most as rewards for excellent performance. They will often tell you exactly what you need to do more of to elicit the very best work from each person.

EIGHT

Install Management by Values

EACH PERSON lives from the inside out. The core of your existence, and the axle around which your entire life turns, is made up of your innermost convictions and your deepest values. It is your values that determine your character and personality. They determine what you stand for and what you will not stand for. One of the marks of superior people is that they are very clear about their values, and they refuse to compromise their values under any circumstances.

You are only really happy when you are living in complete harmony on the outside with your values on the inside. You only perform at your best when your behaviors are congruent with what you believe to be the most valuable principles. On the other hand, stress and tension arise when what you are doing on the outside—your activities and behaviors—are incongruent or out of alignment with what you truly believe on the inside. The best companies recognize that people cannot be motivated to perform tasks or work for an organization whose values are not in harmony with their own.

The Structure of Personality

Imagine that your personality is made up of concentric circles, like a dartboard, beginning with your core values. Your *values* in turn determine the second circle, your *beliefs* about yourself and about reality. You always see your world through the screen of your beliefs, whether valid or invalid, self-limiting or unlimited.

To put it another way, you see the world not as it is, but as you are. As William James of Harvard University once said: "Beliefs create the actual fact."

The third level of your personality, the third concentric circle, is your *expectations*. Just as your values determine your beliefs, your beliefs determine your expectations about yourself, other people, and the world around you. Your expectations become your own self-fulfilling prophecies. Your expectations of others have an inordinate impact on how they behave, especially your expectations of your children, your spouse, and your employees. Your expectations of yourself, whether positive or negative, largely determine how you perform and behave.

Your Attitude Determines Your Personality

Your values, beliefs, and expectations in turn determine your *attitudes* and the way you approach your world. If you

have good values, positive beliefs, and confident expecta
tions, you will have a positive, optimistic attitude towar
yourself and the world around you.

The fifth concentric circle is your *behaviors*. These behav
iors are determined by a combination of your values, you
beliefs, your expectations, and your attitudes.

Action Is Everything

It is not what a person says or wishes or hopes or intends tha
explains who they are inside. It is only the actions that the
take that matter, and especially the actions they take unde
pressure, when they are forced to choose between one actior
and another, between one value and a conflicting value.

Why is this discussion of values so important? The reasor
is that your values are almost a part of your DNA. They are
programmed into you at a deep unconscious level. The
determine your attitude and your behavior, and they seldorr
change throughout life.

The very best companies and managers manage by values
They are very clear about their values and how those values are
expressed in the actions and behaviors of the people in thei
business. They hire as much for character—for a commitmen
to particular values—as they do for competence and ability.

People are happiest working for an organization tha
stands for and practices the values that they personally hold
most dear. Values are everything.

One of my client companies, which started as an idea
and became a national success, began its life with the senior

people sitting down and determining the five values that they would use to govern all of their behaviors and the behaviors of everyone who worked in the organization.

They then defined exactly how they would practice these values in all of their business and personal activities. From then on, whenever they had to make a decision of any kind, they would take out a list of their five values and how those values were to be expressed, and they'd discuss whether the decision was in complete harmony with these guiding principles.

When I worked with this company and attended its annual meeting, I was amazed at how positive, confident, and outgoing the hundreds of people working for the company actually were. They were happy, enthusiastic, and totally committed to the success of the business.

The Fortunate 500

When Ken Blanchard and Norman Vincent Peale elaborated on the Fortunate 500 concept in their book *The Power of Ethical Management*, they discovered that the top 20 percent of businesses in each industry, defined by consistently higher levels of profitability (sometimes ten and twenty times the average in the industry), were all characterized as having clear, written values that everyone knew, believed in, and lived by.

The other companies in the same industries all claimed to have values. These values, however, were either not written down or very few people in the company knew what the values were—much less how the values served as guides to behavior in dealing with people both inside and outside the company.

Meaning and Purpose Make a Difference

The deepest of all human needs, right at the core of personality, is the need for meaning and purpose in life and in work. In your business, meaning and purpose are the answer to the question, "Why do we do what we do in the first place?" When you interview a new employee, be sure to define and describe the work in terms of its meaning and significance to others. What kind of a difference do your products and services make in the lives and work of your customers? How do your products and services change, improve, and transform the lives of other people?

Meaning and purpose always arise from the value structure of the individual. That is why it is so important for you, as a manager, to convey over and over again the values of the organization and what you personally believe in. Values such as quality, integrity, friendliness, service, respect for the individual, personal growth and self-esteem, and social responsibility are factors that trigger, stimulate, motivate, and inspire people.

When people feel that what they are doing serves a higher purpose, that they are making a difference in the lives of other people by the quality of their work, they are motivated to perform at their best.

ACTION EXERCISES

1. Make a list of the three to five most important values upon which you base your business and your decisions. Discuss these values with others and make sure that everyone knows what they are.

2. Define your work in terms of the meaning and purpose it has to you and the difference your products and services make in the lives of your customers. This is the real reason you are in this business in the first place.

NINE

Practice Management by Objectives

MANAGEMENT BY objectives is one of the most powerful and consistent motivators in the world of work. It is a technique first described by Peter Drucker in *Managing for Results*. It refers to the practice of assigning a complete job to a competent individual and then allowing that individual to choose how to complete the task on schedule and on budget.

Four Steps to Management by Objectives

There are four steps to the process of management by objectives:

1. *Get a clear agreement on exactly which goals and objectives are to be accomplished.* This step requires that you be clear about the goal but flexible about the process of achieving it. Management by objectives

requires participatory management and a complete discussion so that there is total agreement between you and the employee about the job to be done.

2. *Discuss with the individual the various ways that the goal might be achieved or the job completed.* Based on your experience, you provide your ideas and input, giving suggestions and advice about the best way to accomplish the task.

3. *Establish clear measurements and benchmarks.* As manager, you need to tell the individual employee exactly how the task will be measured and describe the various benchmarks you will use to ensure that the task is being accomplished on time and on budget.

4. *Agree on a regular schedule to report on progress and get feedback on the job.* You only use management by objectives with competent people who have demonstrated and proven that they are capable of completing a task with little or no supervision. When you have such an employee, you then turn over 100 percent of the responsibility for the attainment of the objective to that person.

Give Them Autonomy and Freedom

Two powerful motivators in the world of work are autonomy and freedom. They go together, hand in hand. People need to stand out as individuals, to be clearly responsible for the completion of important tasks, and to be measured

for individual performance rather than just team performance. At the same time, people want complete freedom
to do the job in their way and on their own schedule.

Freedom and responsibility also go hand in hand. The more
freedom you give people to do their work, the more responsibility they must be willing to take on to get the job done to the
agreed-on standards and by the agreed-on deadline.

When people have proven that they are competent and
capable of a particular task, and they accept complete
responsibility for doing the job, you can give them maximum
freedom; you can actually leave them alone, except for the
occasional times where you check in to measure progress.

Management by objectives is a wonderful time-saver for
a competent executive. The more people you have reporting
to you who are capable of doing their jobs without your
involvement or direct supervision, the more freedom you
have to focus on those tasks that only you can do.
Management by objectives is one of the best ways to build
self-reliance in the people who report to you. It is also one of
the best ways to build self-esteem and self-confidence. When
people are free to work by themselves on a critical job and to
accomplish it in their own way, not only will they be more
creative and motivated, but their self-esteem will go up. And
when they complete the tasks, they will feel like winners.

Don't Take Back the Job

You are the manager and have people reporting to you because
you have probably demonstrated your ability to do many of
the jobs that you now delegate and assign to other people.

Because you have demonstrated competence in doing a particular job, you often find yourself tempted to get involved in the task, even when you have assigned it to someone else. A major weakness in managers is that, after they have been promoted, they often revert back to doing some of their old tasks, those very tasks that should be delegated to others to free up the manager's time for the special responsibilities of the new position.

As manager, you can unintentionally "take the job back" by interfering when someone is working to complete the job you've assigned to him. That can happen if you continually make new suggestions or give direct commands that require the other person to do the job differently from what was agreed on previously. If a problem occurs in carrying out your well-meant instructions, the other person will often stop work on the assignment and wait for you to make another suggestion or decision.

The way that I handle this situation is simple. When employees come to me with a question or concern about a job, I simply ask them, "What do you think we should do?" I force them to think through the problem or obstacle and come up with a suggestion or an idea to solve it or overcome it. Invariably, employees will come back with a suggestion or suggestions about how to go over or around the obstacle. At this point I always say, "That's a good idea."

Then I either encourage them to carry on with the task of implementing the new idea to solve the current problem, or I add a comment or a suggestion about how they might implement *their own idea* even more effectively. But I consciously refuse to interfere with their ability to do the job themselves and with full ownership of the complete task.

As soon as a person demonstrates competence in a particular area, you can begin using management by objectives. Your goal is to push decision making and action as far down the line as possible, thereby freeing your time so that you can do things of higher value. With management by objectives, you can significantly increase the performance, productivity, and output of other people, as well as yourself. You create high levels of motivation in your team members by making the work both challenging and interesting, and by making them completely responsible for getting the job done.

ACTION EXERCISES

1. Look at some of the tasks that are taking up a lot of your time and think about how you could assign them to others, thereby building their confidence and competence and freeing up more of your own time.

2. Create a checklist, based on the recommendations in this chapter, and use it whenever you delegate a complete task to another person. The more competent you become in managing by objectives, the greater freedom and autonomy you give to others and the more freedom you have for yourself.

TEN

Use Management by Exception

YOUR GOAL AS a manager is to unlock the 50 percent of performance that employees have locked up inside of them. You achieve this goal by motivating them to perform at ever-higher levels because they want to, not because they have to. Remember, you cannot motivate anybody from the outside. You can only create the environment that stimulates another person to be motivated internally to do more and better work.

Management by exception (MBE) is a terrific managerial tool to be employed at every opportunity. It is a tremendous motivator of performance because it builds people to higher levels of confidence and competence. MBE also enables you to get much more done and to multiply your personal skills and talents as a manager times almost every person who reports to you.

Let Them Do the Work

Management by exception is used when you assign a job clearly and in its entirety to another person. You and the other person discuss and agree on what is to be accomplished, how it will be measured, and when it is to be achieved. You arrange a schedule to review progress at prearranged intervals, if necessary. You then leave the person alone to do the job, *except* when there is a variance from the agreed-on standards or if something unexpected goes wrong.

The staff member is to report only deviations from the plan. As long as everything is going smoothly, and the job is on schedule, no reporting is necessary. If you do not hear from the person, you are safe to assume that everything is going according to plan.

For example, if you set a specific sales goal such as 1,000 units per week, then the person responsible for the project should come back to you only if weekly sales drop below that 1,000 mark. Other than that, the staff member doesn't have to report to you at all. He has complete freedom and autonomy to do the job, and to get it done in his own way.

With management by exception, you can occasionally check on the job to see how things are going. But as with management by objectives, you must resist the temptation to interfere in any way. The more freedom and responsibility you give employees to do the job in their own way, the more positive and motivated they will be.

As with management by objectives, management by exception can save you a lot of time. When you can free yourself from constantly having to supervise and control a job to be sure that it gets done on schedule, you will have more time for other tasks. And when your staff member completes his task, he'll have the pride and satisfaction of being able to say, "I did it myself."

An excellent manager is someone who continually creates the conditions where employees can feel that they did the job themselves, with minimal instruction, direction, or supervision. As a result, they feel like winners. They feel positive and happy. They are motivated and enthusiastic about doing even more work and accomplishing even more tasks. Confucius once said that the mark of an excellent leader is that, when the job is done, people say, "We did it ourselves." MBE is a tool that you can use regularly to achieve all of these management goals. It is, of course, best used with people of proven competence, the same as with management by objectives. You only want to use this technique when people have demonstrated their ability to do a job consistently and well.

Satisfy the Two Basic Needs

To perform at their best, individuals have two basic needs in the world of work. The first is called "the autonomy need," which is the need to be seen and respected as an individual and to stand out for one's personal performance. It is a need to be recognized for individual achievement, or the "I am special" need.

The second need that each person has in the workplace is "the dependency need." People want to know they are a part of something bigger than themselves. People want to be part of a team. Psychologist Abraham Maslow called it the "affiliation need." It is the need to be recognized and accepted as part of a group of people in the workplace.

Good organizations and good managers create environments where people feel both autonomous and important, on the one hand, but also have their dependency needs satisfied by feeling as if they are part of a team, or part of the larger organization. The reward structures in excellent organizations are designed to reward not only autonomous performance, but also team performance.

Management by objectives and management by exception are two approaches that allow employees to fulfill the basic autonomy need that will motivate them to the highest performance.

ACTION EXERCISES

1. Seek every opportunity to use management by exception with your staff. Give an assignment and tell the staff member that she does not have to report back to you as long as everything is on schedule.

2. Be sure to encourage the staff member to come back to you for your assistance and guidance if, for any reason, something happens that puts the assignment off schedule.

ELEVEN

Apply the
Pareto Principle

ONE OF YOUR most important responsibilities in motivating your people to peak performance is to keep them focused on starting and completing their most important tasks. Important task completion is a major source of energy, enthusiasm, and high self-esteem.

Warren Buffett, the third richest man in the world, had dinner with Bill Gates, the single richest man in the world, and his father, Bill Gates Sr. They were discussing the essential ingredients of success. Almost spontaneously, they all agreed that "focus, focus, focus" is the key to high achievement, especially in business.

Motivation is evident when talented people are working on important tasks and getting them done, one after another. Demotivation occurs when people are inadvertently working on low-value tasks, which contain very little inherent motivational value, and even if they complete these tasks, they get no "bang for the buck."

The 80/20 Rule

The Pareto principle, also known as the 80/20 rule, was discovered by Vilfredo Pareto, an Italian economist, in 1895. After years of research, he concluded that society was made up of two groups of people, which he labeled the *vital few* (the top 20 percent) and the *trivial many* (the bottom 80 percent). Pareto observed that in each society, the top 20 percent of people and families controlled 80 percent or more of the wealth. The bottom 80 percent of people only controlled 20 percent of the wealth.

For more than 100 years, the 80/20 rule has been applied to virtually every area of human activity, and seems to apply to almost all business activities. Twenty percent of your customers will account for 80 percent of your sales and profits. Twenty percent of your products or services will account for 80 percent of your sales activity. Twenty percent of your people will contribute 80 percent of the sales and 80 percent of the results.

The Pareto principle can also be applied to the issue of focusing on important tasks. Accordingly, 20 percent of your activities will count for 80 percent of the value of all those activities, or the total of the results that you will get. This means that if you make a list of ten things that you have to do in a day, two of the items on your list will be worth more than all the others put together.

The Rule of Three

In my work with business owners, executives, and the staff of companies both large and small, I have discovered a "Rule of Three" that is almost completely applicable to work activities. The Rule of Three declares that if you make a list of everything you do in a week or a month—which may be twenty or thirty activities, for the average person—you will find that only *three* of those activities account for fully 90 percent of the value of all the work you do.

In this context, the most important word in the world of work is *contribution*. It is the responsibility of each employee, at whatever level of the enterprise, to make the maximum contribution possible in the hours that he works. And only three activities account for 90 percent of a person's contribution.

How do you discover these three tasks or activities? Simple: You ask the three "magic questions."

IDENTIFY YOUR MOST VALUABLE ACTIVITY

The first question is, "If you could only do *one* thing all day long, which one activity would contribute the most value to your business or organization?"

When you look over the list of things that you do in a week or a month, the task of topmost importance will probably jump out at you. If you are in doubt about the most important thing you do, find out what it is, immediately. Ask your boss for input. Ask your coworkers. Ask yourself. But you absolutely, positively must know the most valuable and important thing that you do.

Then, you ask the question a second time, but in a slightly different way: "If I could only do *two* things all day long, what would be the second most valuable thing that I do?" Your answer will usually become quite clear after a few moments of reflection. You then ask the question one more time: "If I could only do *three* things all day long, what would be number three in terms of making the most valuable contribution?"

Once you have determined your "big three," you then resolve to focus your time and attention on those three activities from the first thing in the morning to the last thing in the evening.

Here's the rule for maximum contribution: Do *fewer* things, but do *more important* things, and do them *more* of the time and *get better* at each one of them.

TEACH THE RULE OF THREE TO OTHERS

One of the most valuable things you can do as a manager is to sit your employees down and help them define their three primary tasks or output responsibilities. Have a meeting where everyone discusses the primary output responsibilities of everyone else. "Peer pressure" is a powerful motivational factor in business. When everyone knows what everyone else is supposed to be doing, and in what order of importance, there is a natural pressure within the organization toward keeping busy on your most important tasks. After all, everyone can quite easily see whether other team members are actually doing the most important things they could be doing to help the team and the company move ahead.

The 80/20 Rule Revisited

For people to enjoy maximum motivation and maximum accomplishment at work, you must make sure that your people are working on the 20 percent of their activities that account for 80 percent of the value of their contribution. Repeat and reaffirm this rule continually to your staff. Set clear priorities for your staff members so that they are always working on those tasks that represent the most valuable use of their time.

One of your jobs as a manager is to teach your people to always be analyzing their work and setting priorities with the Pareto principle and the Rule of Three in mind. Remember, people only feel positive and motivated when they are working on and completing tasks of high value—tasks that make a difference and are recognized and respected as making a valuable contribution to the work.

Avoid Distraction

Today, the greatest enemy of high performance in the world of work is distraction. People are surrounded by too many distracting influences: notifications of newly arrived e-mails, telephone calls on mobile phones, text messages coming through, and especially interruptions by other people who are also living and working in a world of distraction.

Your job is to maximize the performance of your most important and expensive asset—your human resources. You should be continually repeating and reaffirming the importance of your employees working on their most valuable tasks and disciplining themselves to get those tasks completed on time and on budget.

ACTION EXERCISES

1. Make a list of everything you do in the course of a month, and then ask the three magic questions of yourself with regard to your own list of tasks and activities. You should be absolutely clear about the three most important things that you do in the course of a day, week, or month.

2. Bring your staff members together and have all of them bring a list of their activities to the meeting. One by one, help them to clearly define the three most important things they do to make the most valuable contribution to the organization. From then on, encourage people to start and complete their most important tasks before they do anything else.

TWELVE

Be a Teacher

IN MY SEMINARS, I often start off by asking a cryptic question: "What is your most valuable financial asset?"

After a pause while people ponder the question, I tell them, "Your most valuable financial asset is your *earning ability*. It is your ability to get results that people will pay you for."

Of all the assets in a company, only people can be made to appreciate in value. All other assets and resources deteriorate and depreciate over time. When you take the time to grow your people, you can actually cause them to increase in value—in earning and contribution ability—and to increase the value of their work to the organization.

One of your most important roles as a manager is to teach and train the people working under you how to do the job, and how to do the job better. In your role as teacher, you are helping them to feel more valuable and more capable of making an increasingly important contribution to the company, which is also a powerful means of motivating them.

Teaching Is Your Job

When I started off as a manager, I hired people for various positions. They would often come to me and ask for instructions on how to perform a task that I considered to be quite simple or that I thought they should already know how to do. These constant interruptions by my staff were a constant irritation.

Then, one day, I had a revelation: Teaching is not a side issue or a distraction from my work. Instead, it is a key part of my work. The reason I was a manager was because I had already mastered these tasks, so I could then focus and concentrate on tasks of greater complexity and importance. The reason that the members of my staff were working under me was because they did not know how to do these things yet. But they could learn.

Even MBAs Need Instruction

I hired a new MBA graduate some years ago. He was positive and sincere, and he ran marathons. He was obviously not afraid of hard work and was well organized and disciplined.

On his second day, I called him in and asked him to put together a pro forma on a real estate project that we were looking into. He nodded and agreed and went back to his office to begin work. After a couple of days, I asked him how it was going. He looked up at me with a pained expression and said, "Quite honestly, I don't know what a pro forma is."

For me, a pro forma is a simple evaluation of the feasibility of a project or investment. It begins with determining the revenues that can be generated from the project, deducting all costs and expenses of generating those revenues, and arriving at a profit figure. This profit figure is then divided into the cost of the total project in the first place to determine an expected rate of return. Based on this expected rate of return, calculated conservatively, you can determine whether it is a good investment in comparison with other investment opportunities. A pro forma is a basic staple of all business calculations.

But here was this MBA graduate who had no idea of how to put together a pro forma or a financial statement for a business or part of a business. I had falsely assumed that he had been educated on this process and was quite capable of carrying it out. That was my mistake.

Never Assume That People Know

Never assume that your staff members know how to perform difficult or complicated tasks. If they did, they probably wouldn't be working for you in the first place. Rather, it is your responsibility to determine their level of knowledge and experience, and if it is lacking in a particular area, it is your job either to teach and train them personally or to get them the necessary training from other people or outside seminars and workshops.

Take time to instruct, answer questions, and give feedback. One of your most important responsibilities is to teach and "grow" the next generation of managers. Also, by teaching others to perform the tasks that you have already mastered, you free yourself from having to do them personally.

Teaching is a vital activity of the manager. You build the competence and confidence of your staff members and multiply your ability to get the most important results expected of you in your job. Your teaching motivates and inspires people to know that they are becoming more valuable and important to the organization, and thereby increasing their "earning ability" for the long term.

ACTION EXERCISES

1. Identify the important tasks that only you can do today, and then look around you for others you can teach to do these tasks, so that the tasks can become part of their job instead of yours.

2. Take time to ask your staff members what specific skills they would like to learn to be able to make a more valuable contribution to the company. Look for every opportunity to teach, train, and develop people to enable them to get more and better results for the business.

THIRTEEN

Train and Educate Continuously

THE KEY TO motivating your staff members is to create an environment where they feel happy at work. The happier they are, the better work they will do, the more they will cooperate with each other, the more creative they will become, and the more positive a work environment you will have surrounding you.

Earl Nightingale once wrote that "happiness is the progressive realization of a worthy goal, or ideal."

Whenever people believe that they are growing personally, becoming better and better and moving toward becoming the best they could possibly be, they experience happiness and motivation. And nothing can generate these feelings more consistently than your dedication, as a manager, to the continuous training, education, and development of your people.

Continuous learning is the key to high performance, motivation, enthusiasm, and commitment. People will suffer from low self-esteem if they don't know how to accomplish their tasks, which is why teaching is your job (as described in Chapter Twelve). The topic of this chapter, however, is not just about employees learning what they need to know to accomplish their job correctly; it's about your employees continuously learning new things in new areas and continuously upgrading their knowledge and skills, thus opening avenues of personal and professional growth for the future.

The Right Question

Some managers question the idea of training their staff members by asking, "What if we train them and they leave?" That is the wrong question. The right question is, "What if you don't train them and they stay?"

Companies such as IBM and AT&T are passionate about training their people on a regular basis. An employee at IBM, after several months of training prior to beginning work, is required to take forty to eighty additional hours of training each year. This is a minimum requirement for continued employment. Employees take training very seriously.

The best companies spend hundreds of millions of dollars each year training their people because they know that proper training has an incredibly high payoff. According to *Human Resource Executive Magazine*, properly training people in the key skills of their jobs can yield ten, twenty, and even thirty times the cost of the training to the bottom line in subsequent years. For every dollar that a company spends in training, it gets back incredible returns on that investment.

People Are the Greatest Cost

Aside from the cost of goods sold, the average company's operating expenses are about 85 percent payroll and benefits and only 15 percent everything else, including rent and utilities. Even including manufacturing costs, the average company spends 65 percent of its gross revenues on salaries, wages, and associated costs.

According to a study conducted by the American Society for Training and Development, companies spend on average about one percent or less of their gross revenues on training the people who are expected to generate those gross revenues. According to that same study, the top 20 percent of companies in profitability in every industry spend 3 percent or more of their gross sales revenue on training their people. Those companies that spend as much as 5 percent and 10 percent of their gross sales revenues on training consistently achieve the highest growth rates and the highest levels of profitability in their industries.

In a highly competitive market for automotive parts, Dana Corporation was famous for devoting one day per week to training its people in the essential skills they needed to perform their work in an excellent fashion. And the company consistently outperformed and outsold competitors who worked their people five days a week and offered little or no time for training.

Training and Motivation

There is a direct relationship between continuous training and development and the feeling of personal growth and increased self-esteem that people experience. Whenever people take in new information and discover that more of their potential is being released, their self-esteem goes up. Their self-image also improves. They feel happier and more positive about themselves.

One of the jobs of management should be to develop a training plan for each staff member. Sit with the person and determine the skills that she will need, in addition to her existing skills, to make an increasingly more valuable contribution to the business.

If you work for a large company, you can arrange for training internally. If you are employed by a smaller company, there are thousands of excellent training organizations that will come in and conduct specialized training customized for your people and your business. Sometimes, one training program can completely transform the performance of an entire department, or even an entire organization.

Continuous personal and professional growth is the most dependable motivator of people, driving them toward greater levels of competence and higher levels of performance. Training your people is absolutely essential to creating a winning corporate climate.

Training Gives a Competitive Advantage

One senior executive told me, "The only competitive advantage we have is the ability to learn and apply new ideas faster than our competitors."

Just as a top sports team has a rigorous and continuous training program in place, a top company must do the same. The rule is that "your life only gets better when you get better."

By the same token, people only get better when the manager gets better. The company only gets better when the staff gets better. And as Pat Riley, the basketball coach, wrote, "If you're not getting better, you're getting worse." Because of the incredible speed of change and competition in every industry today, if your people and your company are not constantly improving, getting better and better, they are actually falling further and further behind those companies that are training their people to ever higher levels.

Continuous training and development is not a choice. It is not really optional. It is a mandatory activity for survival in the markets of today and tomorrow.

ACTION EXERCISES

1. Ask your people, individually, to determine the one skill that they would like to acquire or improve through training and development to make a more valuable contribution. Then, provide the time and money necessary for each employee to develop that skill.

2. Select one skill for yourself that can help you to do your job even better. Set up a personal training schedule of reading, listening to audio programs, attending seminars and workshops, and *practicing* your new skill in the workplace. Your example will serve as motivation and an inspiration to other people to upgrade their skills as well.

FOURTEEN

Insist on the Zero Defects Principle

FULLY 90 PERCENT of business success will be determined by your ability to produce a great product or service in the first place. The PIMS (Profit Impact of Marketing Strategy) studies, conducted at Harvard over many years and embracing hundreds of companies, demonstrated that there is a direct relationship between the perceived quality of the product or service you produce and the profitability of your organization.

The most profitable companies—the ones that can charge the highest prices and earn the highest profit margins—are always those that are perceived in the market as being the highest-quality providers in their areas of business activity.

It is the same with individuals. If you want people to feel like winners, you must create an environment where they are encouraged to win. And winning in the world of work largely means doing work of excellent quality and being recognized for that work.

Quality Is Free

Philip Crosby, at his Quality College and in his book *Quality Is Free*, defined quality this way: "Quality means that the product or service you sell does what you said it would do when the customer bought it, and continues to do it. Your quality rating is determined by the percentage of times that your product continues to deliver on its promises."

The highest quality rating is called "zero defects." This rating means that your product or service *always* does what you said it would do when you sold it to your customer. By the same token, individuals can receive a *personal quality* rating. When people always do their jobs in an excellent fashion 100 percent of the time, consistently over time, they also earn a "zero defects" rating.

With the zero defects principle, you encourage everyone to concentrate on doing quality work and producing quality products and services. If you are the leader of the company, you make an organizationwide commitment to excellence. You get every employee to continually think in terms of doing an excellent job, every time.

SET HIGH-QUALITY STANDARDS

By initiating the zero defects concept, you set a standard of 100 percent quality. This means no mistakes and no defects. You want to make a big deal out of the quality work of each individual. Acknowledge, reward, recognize, and reinforce quality whenever you see it.

It is said that people tend to perform at their best under the most demanding of bosses. The boss sets the tone for the whole organization. That's why the boss's attitude toward quality and excellence will set the standard for everyone else.

SEND IT BACK

There is a famous story told about Henry Kissinger when he was secretary of state. He asked a subordinate to produce a report on an important national issue. The subordinate brought him the report, and Kissinger said that he would look at it and talk to him about it the following day.

When the subordinate came in the following day, Kissinger gave him the report back and said that it was not yet good enough and that he could do a much better job if he took a little bit more time to polish and perfect it. The subordinate went away to work on it again for the next two or three days.

Once more, he brought the report back to Kissinger, who again reviewed it overnight. The following day, Kissinger returned the report to the subordinate and said that it was still not good enough. He would have to work even harder to polish the report for it to be of sufficient quality. Once again, the subordinate took the report away and worked on it for another two or three days.

Finally, the subordinate returned to Kissinger with the report. This time, he said that it was the very best report he could possibly write. There was nothing he could do to improve it in any way. If Kissinger was not satisfied with the report in its current form, the subordinate said, there was nothing he could do to make it any better.

At this, Kissinger replied, "Well, if you are completely convinced that it cannot be any better, I will now read it for the first time."

SET A GOOD EXAMPLE

In addition to demanding high standards of quality in the work of each person, you must set an example of high-quality work yourself. You lead the way. You are the role model. When you do excellent work—work that is obviously the result of "going the extra mile"—you set a standard for everyone who works for you and with you.

Every time a person does an excellent job, his self-esteem goes up. Every time people do an average job and others accept it, their self-esteem remains unaffected. And when they do a poor job that is allowed to pass, their self-esteem actually goes down. When people do poor-quality work, they feel a little bit inferior and a lot like losers in the world of work.

When someone does an excellent job and is recognized, rewarded, and appreciated for doing so, that person feels like a winner. But very few people can do an excellent job unless someone sets a standard of superior quality for them and then holds them to that standard. Zero defects is a wonderful target to aim for.

The Value of Quality Work

Going back to our previous discussion about values (in Chapter Eight), it is important that you explain to your staff members that the survival and success of your business is dependent on the quality of the work that you produce. Encourage them to strive to do a perfect job every time. Even in small things, such as writing a letter, an e-mail, or advertising copy, little things mean a lot. By insisting that every piece of correspondence or communication from the company is letter-perfect, carefully proofed, and edited so that there are no mistakes, you set a standard of excellence that permeates and spreads through the entire organization.

Accuracy, precision, and perfection are essential when producing a proposal for a customer or completing an order form for a purchase or sale. When people receive any form of written correspondence from your organization, they immediately judge the entire quality of the company—including its products, services, and people—by the accuracy and mistake-free nature of the communication.

When one of your employees does something of superior quality, make it a big deal. Remember, you're going to get more of whatever you recognize, reward, and reinforce. When you constantly remind people of the importance of doing excellent quality work, you set an ideal that more and more of your people will aspire to. As they aspire to ever-higher ideals of quality work, their self-image improves and their self-esteem goes up. They are even more motivated to do even better work in the future.

ACTION EXERCISES

1. Set standards of excellent performance for every job, product, or service that goes to your customers, and make sure that each person on your staff knows exactly what they are.

2. Set an example by doing high-quality work yourself, in every area, and by continually striving to become even better at the most important things you do.

FIFTEEN

Introduce Quality Circles, Quality Teams

ALL WORK IS done by teams. The output of the manager is actually the output of the team. The more efficiently and effectively the team works together, the higher the quality and quantity of production, and the better the manager looks to everyone, especially to superiors.

Quality circles are a Japanese management technique developed in the 1960s and 1970s by W. Edwards Deming, who helped make Japan a recognized world leader in quality products. By forming people into quality circles and quality teams, you encourage and motivate them to take greater responsibility for improving the quality of everything they do.

Quality teams and quality circles only work, however, when they receive clear, explicit support from top management. They cannot be used as a gimmick or device to motivate people unless the managers make it clear that every quality initiative is an extremely important activity for the company and for its sales and profitability in the future.

Staff Members Only

Quality teams are assembled by management but consist only of staff members. Each team is composed of peers who select their own leader for the group. The job of the team members is to get together once a week on company time to talk about ways that they can improve the quality of their work and the way the business operates in their area of responsibility.

Quality teams should be encouraged to meet during regular work hours to address specific questions and problems that require concrete, practical answers. Quality teams should also meet interdepartmentally to brainstorm for ideas on how to improve product quality, order handling and processing, inventory handling, and other areas that affect customers and company reputation.

The U.S. equivalent of the Deming Prize for quality—the highest award that a company can receive in Japan—is the Baldrige Award. This award was set up under President Ronald Reagan and named for his then secretary of commerce, Malcolm Baldrige.

Each year, American companies strive to earn the Baldrige Award. To be considered, they must complete a fifty- to sixty-page questionnaire describing every detail of their current business operations. If this questionnaire is satisfactory to the Baldrige Award judges, usually consisting of senior executives of companies that have won the award in previous years, the company is then subject to a rigorous quality audit.

Management by Measurement

Over the years, the Baldrige Awards have focused on what is called "management by measurement." Every activity of the company is broken down into numbers and then carefully measured and compared against previous and current performance, and the performance of other organizations in the same field. The goal is to continually improve the numbers that indicate quality in a particular area of activity by carefully monitoring those numbers.

When people have clear target numbers to improve, they are internally motivated to find better, faster, easier, and more creative ways to do the job better in every area. By assembling quality teams and quality circles to focus on continuous improvement, management creates an internal pressure toward superior performance that is both motivating and liberating for the individuals involved in the process.

In the best companies, everyone in the organization, at every level, is involved in a quality team of some kind. Every activity that affects the sales, profitability, and customer satisfaction of the business is continuously studied and scrutinized while seeking ways to make it better and better.

Once the quality team has met and come up with ideas and recommendations for quality improvement, the group leader reports to management in writing on these recommendations.

The X Factor Revisited

When team members are continually solicited for their opinions and ideas on how to improve the quality of the work, they feel more valuable and important and, therefore, more motivated to do even better work in the future.

Remember the X factor. The self-image of employees is greatly influenced by the way they are treated by their managers and the executives of the company. If they are respected by the organization's leaders, they will view themselves in a more positive way and, as a result, perform at higher levels. Participation in a quality team or a quality circle is a tangible indication that the organization values their contribution. When employees know that they are listened to and respected by the company, they take their jobs and the quality of their work far more seriously.

Quality teams are also effective motivators because they fulfill the two basic human needs as discussed in Chapter Ten: the affiliation need and the autonomy need. As humans, we want both autonomy and affiliation; we are at once motivated by a sense of independence yet energized and encouraged by being members of a team. Although they are advisory in nature, quality teams are self-directed, allowing employees to meet among themselves and generate new ideas and initiatives to improve the quality of the product and services of the company. Members of quality teams and quality circles enjoy both the freedom of staff-only teams as well as the motivation of group participation.

ACTION EXERCISES

1. Select one area in your business that affects customer satisfaction and form a quality team to make recommendations to improve the company's performance in that area.

2. Set specific measures of quality in each important area of the business, and then look for ways to practice continuous and never-ending improvement (CANEI) in each of those areas.

SIXTEEN

Practice Brainstorming Regularly

BRAINSTORMING is one of the fastest ways to unleash creative thinking and build motivation in any organization. As a manager, it is one of the most important tools that you can use to solve problems, overcome obstacles, achieve business goals, and build a powerful team of highly committed people.

The brainstorming process was first described by Alex Osborn, an advertising executive, in 1946. Over the years, it has been developed and improved so that it is now used on a regular basis in all fast-growing, competitive organizations. If you are not now using brainstorming to propel your business forward, it is quite an easy thing to begin.

The purpose of brainstorming is to unleash the creativity of everyone within your organization. And you will often be happily surprised. Sometimes, staff members who aren't particularly outgoing or talkative turn out to have incredible ideas that can have a profound impact on the results of your business.

A Brainstorming Exercise

Some years ago, IBM asked me to conduct a series of problem-solving and decision-making seminars across the country, which I did over the following year. In this one-day seminar program, one of the exercises was to teach the brainstorming process. Seminar participants sat at round tables, with six or seven people per table. I would then assign them exercises that they did in cooperation with one another.

In the brainstorming exercise, the participants had to come up with as many ideas as possible to solve a particular problem. In this case, the problem was that a brick factory had overproduced thousands of bricks that it could not sell in the current market. The factory was looking for different ways to use bricks other than in walls held together with cement or mortar. The participants had twenty minutes to come up with the greatest number of ideas possible. They would all be competing against each other table for the *highest number* of ideas or answers they could generate.

At each table, one person was assigned to write down the ideas as fast as people could come up with them. Groups of people of the same relative rank and job title were at each table. Some tables consisted exclusively of managers or executives; others consisted of technical people. One table, I remember, was composed of seven secretaries, all women.

Quantity vs. Quality

I traveled around the country for IBM giving the seminar, and the average number of answers that a table would come up with in the course of this brainstorming exercise was seventy to eighty ideas. But in this particular seminar, the table consisting only of secretaries came up with more than 200 ideas on how to dispose of this oversupply of bricks. They came up with so many ideas in twenty minutes that they had to have three of the seven women sitting at the table writing down the answers. They turned out to be far more creative than tables full of senior managers or other executives.

The point is that you must never underestimate the creative capability of your staff members. Sometimes, a single person will have an idea or insight that can change the direction of your business, as long as you tap into the creative capacity of that person.

The Seven Parts of the Brainstorming Process

1. *Choose an optimum group size.* The ideal group size for brainstorming is four to seven people. Fewer than four or more than seven people will either not yield enough ideas or will not give each person an opportunity to make a maximum contribution.

2. *Select both a leader for the table and a recorder.* The job of the leader is to keep the session moving, making sure that everybody gets a chance to contribute and that no one dominates the conversation. The job of the recorder is to write down the

ideas as fast as they are generated. Have participants at the table make their selections before the
brainstorming session begins.

3. *Set a specific time limit for the brainstorming session.* Somewhere between fifteen and forty-five
   minutes is recommended. Start and stop punctu-
   ally. When people have a time limit, they tend to
   focus far more quickly and contribute better ideas,
   and more of them.

4. *Define a specific problem or question that demands
   practical answers.* "How can we increase customer
   response times?" is far better than asking, "How can
   we make customers happier?" The more specific the
   question, the more valuable will be the answers.

5. *Focus on quantity of ideas rather than the quality of
   ideas.* Make it a game or a contest to generate as
   many ideas as possible, as fast as possible, within the
   time period allowed for the brainstorming sessions.

6. *Suspend all judgment.* Concentrate on generating
   ideas, period. Don't ridicule, comment on, or evaluate any of the ideas during the brainstorming session. Encourage wild ideas, humor, and thinking
   "outside the box." Build on the ideas of others. Add
   to the ideas of others. Combine ideas to come up
   with even more ideas. If the participants are not
   laughing and enjoying themselves during the session, something is wrong.

7. Gather up all the ideas generated for evaluation at a later time. This step ensures that there will be no ego investments in being "right" or in having one's personal ideas given more weight than those of another participant.

How Brainstorming Works

Once each table generates from fifty to eighty ideas in answer to a specific question, stop the exercise and take a break. After the break, have each recorder pass the ideas from that table to the leader at the next table. The leader then leads an exercise to discuss and evaluate the quality of each of the ideas generated by the other table.

In this situation, there is *no ego involvement*, because no one at the table had contributed any of the ideas under discussion. At the end of the session, the very best ideas, determined by consensus, are then presented to the whole group by each table.

I've used this format even when there are eight or more people involved in the brainstorming session. You can then divide these people into two or more groups, and have each group evaluate the ideas generated by one of the other groups.

The Benefits of Brainstorming

The benefits of brainstorming are numerous. Brainstorming builds involvement, commitment, loyalty, and enthusiasm. Participating in the sessions stimulates and unlocks people's creative talents. Brainstorming also builds self-esteem because people are being asked for their participation and their ideas.

With brainstorming, you can create a better climate for cooperation and teamwork. You encourage better friendships and communication when people engage in brainstorming activities together. The most important payoff is that you will come up with lots of good ideas and sometimes ideas that change the direction of the business. In my experience, brainstorming exercises have resulted in a series of first-rate ideas to increase the sales and profitability of an organization.

It is a primary responsibility of managers to hold brainstorming sessions on a regular basis. If you are not now doing it, you are neglecting an extremely powerful management tool and wasting the untapped brainpower of your most precious company resources.

When you conduct brainstorming sessions regularly, such as once a week, you will be astonished at the number of good ideas that the average person can generate to help you do your job and operate your company better.

ACTION EXERCISES

1. Resolve today to conduct one brainstorming session as outlined and explained in this chapter. Write out the instructions on a piece of paper so that everyone knows exactly what to do and how to do it.

2. From now on, whenever you have a question or a problem in your business, quickly assemble a brainstorming team for fifteen to forty-five minutes to focus and concentrate on developing the greatest number of ideas possible to solve the problem. You may be astonished at the results.

SEVENTEEN

Become a Mentor

NOBODY DOES IT alone. Each person who is successful today is successful as a result of the ideas, input, wisdom, and guidance of people they have met throughout their careers. Sometimes this mentoring is direct: one-on-one private sessions aimed at helping the individual to identify areas for improvement and to implement new ideas and skills in that area.

Sometimes mentoring is *indirect*. It comes from working with senior people possessed of greater wisdom and experience, and learning from those people by observing how they do their jobs and handle their responsibilities. The best mentor I ever had personally was a senior executive who never mentored me at all. Instead, he let me sit in on meetings where significant issues were discussed and important decisions were made. The things I learned from watching him in action still affect me today.

Take an Active Interest

One of the most powerful motivational factors in the world of work is for you to take an active interest in the careers of the people who report to you. Because you are busy, you probably do not have enough time to sit and chat with junior employees for long periods. Instead, you can be a mentor in short bursts of a few minutes by taking the time to give a little guidance and point them in the right direction.

If you are serious about becoming a mentor, take the time to pick one or two people in your company and then become a guide, friend, coach, and counselor to them. They can be people under you or near you, or even in other departments. One of your key functions as a senior manager is to bring along young, talented, and ambitious people, helping them and guiding their careers.

The wonderful thing about mentoring is that attention from a respected senior person can build an individual's self-esteem and self-confidence. The individual being mentored will feel more important and valuable, and will grow more dedicated and committed to the work and to the company. Individual attention from a senior person is a major motivator of personal growth and performance.

Paying Attention Is Paying Value

There is a basic rule that whenever we pay attention to someone, we are also paying value to that person. We are helping to raise another person's self-esteem and making the person feel more important. When you pay this kind of value to junior members of your staff by taking an active interest in their lives and futures, they become more loyal and committed to you, and they do a better job.

Many successful executives today repeatedly report that it was having another executive take an interest in their progress that made all the difference in their lives and careers. It can be the same for you.

One of the greatest tributes to your success as a manager will be the number of people who say that you are the person who made them what they are today. Many senior managers find that they get their greatest satisfaction in life from following the progress of the people they have mentored over the years.

Key Considerations in Mentoring

Mentoring, however, is not as simple as selecting junior people and giving them regular advice to help them in their careers. The first consideration is always that of compatibility or chemistry. For a mentor-mentee relationship to work, the two must be relaxed and comfortable with each other.

I have sought out mentors in the past, and at the first meeting realized that we were not a good fit. The other person and I did not get along comfortably. It was gradually clear to both of us that we wouldn't have a good mentor-mentee relationship.

People have approached me to be their mentor in the past as well. In some cases, I have been a mentor to those people for months and even years. In other cases, after the first meeting, it was clear that there was no rapport between us, and the mentor relationship never got off the ground.

TAKE YOUR TIME

If you are seeking a mentor-mentee relationship with a person above you, start with a cup of coffee and explain to the person that you would very much appreciate occasional input and guidance in your career. If the mentor is open to this idea, and the two of you are compatible, be sure that you do not overwhelm the other person with time demands. Keep your mentoring sessions to ten minutes.

When you meet with your mentor, have a list of questions, concerns, or observations that you would like to discuss. Be sure that you have a copy for your mentor. When your mentor gives you recommendations of books to read or courses to take, be sure to take action on those recommendations immediately. Report back to your mentor what you did and what you learned. You want to reinforce to your mentor that spending time with you is a good investment in the future.

INSTRUCT YOUR MENTEE

When you become a mentor, explain these general rules and guidelines for effective mentoring to the other person. Have the mentee come to you with a written list of questions or concerns. Schedule your meetings in ten-minute blocks or longer if you have the time. Have a specific starting and stopping time. Be punctual for the meeting, and end the meeting at the time agreed.

Parkinson's Law says, "Work expands to fill the time allotted for it." If you allocate ten or fifteen minutes to a mentoring session, and the mentee is aware of that, you will be happily surprised at how quickly you get through all the items on the list in that short period of time.

Both being a mentor and being a mentee can be greatly enriching experiences in your life. As a mentor to junior staff members, you can often have an influence on them that will last for many years, if not their entire lifetimes.

ACTION EXERCISES

1. Select one person on your team who shows excellent potential and take the time to meet with that individual for ten minutes at least once a week. Offer to help with this individual's career in any way possible.

2. Look around you and select someone you like and admire who is more knowledgeable and experienced than you in your field. Get together with this person for coffee and ask if you can call for advice once or twice a month. This can be the beginning of a beautiful friendship.

EIGHTEEN

Lead by Example

ONE OF THE most important responsibilities of management is to lead by example and to be a role model for members of the staff. It is to help them shape their self-ideal by being the kind of person that they admire and respect.

Leading by example is an absolute requirement in management, and a prerequisite for leadership. The character and performance among people in the workplace can never be higher or better than the behaviors, standards, and integrity of the management, including you.

You do not *raise* morale in an organization. Morale filters down from the top. It is based on the character and personality of the leader or manager. The words and actions of the manager set the tone of the entire department, whether positive or negative, productive or unproductive.

The Great Question

One of the great questions for you to ask is: "What kind of company would my company be if everyone in it was just like me?"

In business, it is generally accepted that employees treat customers the way they are treated by their managers. Whenever you experience excellent customer service, you know that there is an excellent manager behind the scenes who takes very good care of his people. Whenever you experience poor customer service, you know that there is a poor or negative manager that these people report to. Since they cannot pay their manager back for the negative way they are being treated, they simply take it out on the customers. You see this all the time.

The key is for you to adopt a warm, friendly, and supportive personality around your people. You create a positive corporate climate by being a positive, cheerful, and confident person.

At work, the boss (and everything the boss does) has an inordinate influence on the thoughts, feelings, attitudes, and behaviors of the staff. A positive or encouraging word from the boss can make a person feel happy and more productive all day long. On the other hand, a negative comment or a frown from the boss can cause a person to become anxious, insecure, and generally less productive for the rest of the day. The things that you do and say as a manager have a major impact on other people.

Everyone Is Watching

Everybody watches the boss, all the time. People watch you out of the corner of their eye. Whatever you say to anyone is quickly relayed to everyone else. And everyone knows everything. There are no secrets in a business or an organization. If you make a positive or negative comment about someone, even casually, it will come back to that person faster than you can imagine—and usually as a distortion of what you really said.

In meetings, you are on display. Everyone is watching you. People are aware of everything you do or say, and even the things that you neglect to do or say.

One of the best ways to lead by example is to always be positive. Always speak in a positive and uplifting way about each staff member when you are talking to other staff members. Whenever you compliment other people behind their backs, it will get back to them quite quickly and have the desired effect of raising their self-esteem and improving their self-image.

The Testing Time

The most important time for you to set an example is when things go wrong—when you are under pressure, when there is a major problem, reversal, or setback in the organization. This is called the "testing time," and it's when and where you demonstrate the real quality of your character. This is when you show everyone who you really are inside.

In 2010, I was diagnosed with throat cancer. For someone who has built a twenty-person business around professional speaking engagements, seminars, and video/audio record-ings, the discovery that I had throat cancer was a real shock.

At the same time, I realized that all of my staff members would be affected by my diagnosis, especially in wondering if their jobs were safe and secure. People think about their incomes all the time.

Fortunately, I had excellent doctors, and the cancer was one that was eminently treatable. My doctors had caught it at stage one, and although I required chemotherapy, surgery, and radiation to deal with it, I was not in any danger of losing my life.

As soon as I understood the gravity of my situation (or lack of), I made it a habit to go into my office and talk to each person every week. I remained continually positive, upbeat, and cheerful. I told them what was going on, my course of treatment, what was likely to happen, when I would lose my voice and for how long, and every other detail.

As a result, although people were worried, they continued to be positive and carried on the business of the company as though everything was quite normal.

An Opportunity to Demonstrate Character

Whenever you have a problem or a crisis in your business, remember that everyone is watching you. This is an oppor-tunity for you to demonstrate your qualities and character as a leader. Your job is not to react negatively or with any kind of panic to negative situations, but to respond calmly and effectively, and to keep everybody focused on solutions and on doing a good job.

As the leader, if you want other people to be effective, efficient, and punctual, you must also be effective, efficient, and punctual. Manage your time well. Set clear priorities, work on your most important tasks, and demonstrate diligence and industriousness at your work for all to see. You cannot expect other people to perform at any higher level than you perform on a day-to-day basis.

Also, as the manager, be courageous and decisive. Be willing to take principled positions, stand up for your staff, and make firm decisions. And be able to explain the reasons for the things that you do. Just imagine that every day and in every way your staff is watching you and forming its own behaviors by observing the way you act. Set a good example for everyone on your staff so that if every employee behaved the way you do, your company would be a terrific place to work.

ACTION EXERCISES

1. Select one behavior that you can change in order to demonstrate your quality and character as a manager—a behavior that would be helpful for everyone to practice (such as punctuality).

2. Resolve today to remain calm, positive, and cheerful whenever something goes wrong, because everyone will be watching.

NINETEEN

Listen to Your Staff

LEADERS ARE LISTENERS. The best leaders listen twice as much as they talk. They have a very high question-to-talk ratio. They ask a lot of questions of their staff and give them an opportunity to express themselves openly and honestly on a regular basis.

You can tell the quality of the relationship between the manager and employees by how freely employees express their ideas and opinions to the manager without fear of being criticized or ignored.

In the annual studies of GreatPlacetoWork.com, one of the most important characteristics of the best companies is that they have high levels of *trust*. Trust means, "I can speak my opinions freely to my managers without fear of being criticized or losing my job."

Listening Is Powerful

Listening has been called "white magic" because it has an almost magical effect on making people feel terrific about themselves. When you listen to other people, you "pay value" to them and make them feel more important and worthwhile.

On average, managers spend 60 percent or more of their time in meetings and conversation with staff members and superiors. The more and the better you listen, the more aware you will be of what is going on, the faster you will sense problems or difficulties that you can help to resolve, and the more relaxed and confident your people will be in your presence.

Four Keys to Effective Listening

The four key skills, which you'll learn here, are (1) listening attentively, (2) pausing, (3) asking questions to get clarification, and (4) paraphrasing.

LISTEN ATTENTIVELY

Lean forward and listen closely to what the other person is saying. Put aside all distractions. Turn off your telephone and shut off the sound on your computer. When you sit and talk with a staff member, treat that person as if he is the most important person in the world.

It is said that "rapt attention is the highest form of flattery." When you listen intently to people, it has a physical effect on them. Their heart rate increases, their galvanic skin response goes up, and their blood pressure increases. When you listen intently to people, making them feel more valuable and important, their self-esteem and self-confidence increase.

Lean forward, look at the person's face intently, and flick your eyes occasionally to meet the other person's eyes. Nod, smile, and be an active listener. Let the other person know that what she is saying is important to you and that you are paying very close attention to it.

Most of all, do not interrupt or even attempt to interrupt. Most people are so concerned with their next comment that they barely listen to one another. They merely wait for an opportunity to jump in when the other person takes a breath.

PAUSE BEFORE REPLYING

When the other person stops talking, instead of immediately commenting, allow a silence to develop in the conversation. A brief silence of no more than three to five seconds gives you three advantages:

1. When you pause, you are telling people that you are carefully considering what they've said, which makes them feel more valued and respected.

2. When you pause, you avoid the risk of interrupting other people if they are just reorganizing their thoughts before continuing.

3. When you pause, you actually hear the other person's meaning at a deeper level of mind. Remember, it is not only what people say, but what they don't say that is essential to the message they are conveying.

The very best listeners practice the "art of the pause" in every conversation. It gives them a tremendous advantage in both understanding others and in being understood.

QUESTION FOR CLARIFICATION

Never assume what people really mean by what they are saying. Instead, if there is any ambiguity, simply ask, "How do you mean?" This question is the most powerful question ever discovered for guiding and directing a conversation.

People are conditioned from early childhood to respond whenever they are asked a question. When you say, "How do you mean," people will almost invariably answer by expanding on their previous comments, giving you more material to enable you to understand clearly what they really mean.

Remember, *the person who asks questions has control.* The person answering the questions is controlled by the person who is asking the questions. The more questions you ask, the more control you have over the conversation, in a very positive way. The more you ask questions, the more you learn and understand—and the more information you acquire that enables you to make better decisions and to be a better manager.

PARAPHRASE THE SPEAKER'S WORDS

Reiterate what the person has just said and paraphrase it in your own words. This is the "acid test" of listening. This is where you demonstrate that you were *really* listening closely to what the other person was saying, rather than smiling politely while being preoccupied with your own thoughts.

You can say something like, "Let me make sure I understand exactly where you're coming from . . . ," and then go on to rephrase what the other person has just said. When the other person agrees that, yes, you really do understand what she was trying to say, you can then reply with your own comments or observations.

Listening Builds Trust

Asking questions is the key to leadership and to good communications. When you ask questions, you get a chance to listen to the answers. And listening builds trust. Trust between two people is the foundation of peak performance.

Even more important, listening builds character. The more you listen to other people and genuinely try to understand and empathize with them, the more you develop yourself. It requires tremendous discipline, after all, to listen attentively without interrupting. Practice listening patiently, unhurriedly, and in a relaxed way. Listen as if you have all the time in the world. Remember that some people need more time to get to the point than others.

When people feel that they can speak openly and honestly in front of their bosses, and their bosses focus their entire attention on attempting to understand what they are saying, those bosses are communicating to employees that they value their people, care about them, and consider them to be important. Listening attentively to other people is a powerful motivational tool that not only builds them up, but it also builds you up, making you a better and better informed manager. Listening enables you to get a true understanding of what your people are thinking and feeling.

ACTION EXERCISES

1. Resolve today that when someone wants to speak with you, you will close the door, shut off your cell phone, and eliminate any disturbances so that you can focus single-mindedly on the other person.

2. Practice asking more questions and then listening attentively to the answers, without commenting or interrupting. Listening intently to another person is the very best way to build trust between the two of you, and trust is the foundation of morale and peak performance in the workplace.

TWENTY

Remember the Friendship Factor

WHEN EMPLOYEES were surveyed about the characteristics of the best bosses they ever had, they almost universally replied by saying, "I always felt as though the boss cared about me as a person, rather than just as a member of the staff."

The friendship factor is an important relationship quality that leads to and enables people to perform at their very best. Establishing high levels of friendship among the staff and between the staff and the manager is the key to success in business today. The quality of the interaction between the employer and the employee is the vital determinant of motivation and performance in any organization. The existence or nonexistence of the friendship factor will determine how helpful and cooperative your staff will be when it comes to working for you, with you, and with the other team members to get the job done.

In a larger sense, it is safe to say that your success in business is going to be proportional to the number and quality of business friendships that you develop throughout your career. It is not just the number of people you know, but the number of people who know you in a positive way. The more people know *and like* you, the more open they will be to voluntarily helping you in your life and work.

The existence of the friendship factor has a huge impact on whether your employees perform at a higher level of quality, achieve excellence, and feel terrific about themselves when working with you.

Practice Clarity and Consideration

Excellent managers seem to have a balance of two important qualities: clarity and consideration. They express caring, concern, and compassion with their employees, treating them like members of their corporate family and making them feel happy and secure in their work. At the same time, they are absolutely crystal clear with regard to tasks, outputs, and the responsibilities of each person. All employees know exactly what is expected of them to do the job well.

The friendship factor is developed with the three Cs: consideration, caring, and courtesy. These are the normal behaviors of excellent managers toward the people who report to them.

You practice *consideration* with your staff when you ask them about themselves, and especially about their families and their personal lives. When you show an interest in what they are doing outside of work, you are telling them that you value them as individuals who have lives that are separate and apart from the workplace. When you ask people about their personal lives, and listen attentively to the answers, they feel more valuable and important, and as a result they like and respect you even more.

Care About Your Staff

You express *caring* for your staff members when they tell you of a problem and you immediately stop and make an effort to help them to solve the problem in some way.

For example, I always tell my employees, "Children come first." By this, I mean that if any of their children ever has a need or problem of any kind while they are at work, they can leave immediately to take care of the child without any deduction of pay or requirement to make up the time. For young mothers, this is one of the very best ways for an employer to show that you really care for them and the most important parts of their lives.

When you ask employees questions about their families and their personal lives and express sympathy for the challenges they face, you demonstrate that you genuinely care. You also show caring and consideration by being appreciative and complimenting them on their possessions, clothes, and personal achievements.

Practice Golden Rule Management

You express *courtesy* toward your staff when you show personal regard and respect for each person. When you maintain a courteous demeanor—especially under stress, when a situation goes wrong, or when an employee has a problem—you increase your people's feelings of security and comfor in the workplace. When you are courteous to people, it lead to improved morale and higher motivation.

The key to the friendship factor is for you to practice what is called the "Golden Rule of Management." Treat other people the way you would like to be treated by your superiors. Treat your staff members as if they are partners or clients—as essential, valued parts of the enterprise.

When Jack Welch was CEO of General Electric, he encouraged all managers to treat their staff members as though those same staff members would be managers over them the following year. Because of the competitive nature of General Electric, and the rapid promotion of highly competent people, it was not uncommon for people to find themselves working under a person who had been under them not long ago. This potential change of positions caused everyone within General Electric to treat one another exactly as they would want to be treated if the roles were reversed.

The Best Time of Your Work Life

The very best time in your work life is when you will be getting along the best with your boss. The very worst time in your work life is when you are having difficulties or problems with your boss. Your job as a manager is to make sure that you are getting along well with all of your employees and they are all getting along well with you.

It is quite easy to practice the Golden Rule in your behavior toward your staff. You can simply ask yourself some key questions, such as:

- What causes me to feel the very best about myself when I am at work? What makes me happy, excited, enthusiastic, and fulfilled at work?

- Who are the best bosses I have ever had, and what did they do or say to me that made me feel happy about my work? How can I create this same positive feeling among the people who report to me?

- What is the ideal relationship that I would like to have with my coworkers?

Whatever your answers to these questions, use them as a guide to the way you treat your own staff. Do and say the same things to other people that you would want them to do and say to you, if the positions were reversed.

ACTION EXERCISES

1. Each day, in your first communication with staff members, ask them about themselves, their personal lives, and their families. Listen attentively to the answers, nodding, smiling, and expressing both interest and sympathy. Only then should you begin talking about work.

2. Practice the Golden Rule of Management on every occasion. When you talk to a staff member, imagine that he or she will be your boss in a short time, and only you know about it.

TWENTY-ONE

Create Motivational Magic

YOUR SUCCESS AS a manager will be determined by your ability to elicit extraordinary performance from ordinary people. Your goal is to build a winning team of highly motivated people who will give their very best toward the achievement of the objectives of the organization.

There are seven behaviors that you can practice every day to motivate your people to perform at their very best and unleash the untapped 50 percent of capacity that most people bring with them to work and take home again at the end of the day. (Each of these behaviors is more fully explained in my book *Full Engagement*, AMACOM, 2011.)

1. *Smile.* When you see someone for the first time each day, smile at that person. Look people squarely in the face, pause, and smile, making it clear that you are happy to see them. It takes just thirteen muscles to smile and 112 muscles to frown. So it is much easier to smile at people when you see them each day. And it makes them feel happy and motivated.

2. *Ask people questions.* Talk to them; ask them questions about how they are doing today and how everything is going. When you express a genuine interest in other people, it makes them feel valuable, respected, and important. They will feel good inside and will want to please you by doing a good job.

3. *Listen to them.* Listen attentively when people talk to you. When you listen to people closely, without interruption, it makes them feel valuable and raises their self-esteem. Being intensely listened to by the boss actually releases endorphins in people's brains, which cause them to feel happier and better about themselves. When you listen, be sure to nod, smile, and watch the person's face intently. Show that whatever the person is saying is of great interest and importance to you. Active listening only takes a few moments each day, but it has a powerful, positive effect on how people do their jobs.

4. *Be polite.* Always be polite, courteous, and respectful when you talk with your staff members. Treat them as if they are talented, intelligent, and accomplished. Lean forward and face them directly, as if there is nothing in the world you would rather do than interact with them at this moment.

5. *Say "thank you."* For everything they do, small or large, thank people. Thank them for being at the meeting on time, for completing an assignment, for giving you a piece of information, and for any other thing that they do that is part of their job. Expressing appreciation toward other people, thanking them for something they have done or said, is another way of making them feel more valuable and important.

6. *Keep people informed.* Keep them fully informed of the company, the business, and especially anything that is going on that may have an impact on their work or their job security. The most satisfied employees in every organization report that they feel that they are insiders, that they are "in the know," and that they are aware of everything that is going on around them that affects them or their work in any way.

7. *Encourage continuous improvement.* Encourage people to come up with ideas to do their jobs better or to improve the company in any way possible. The Japanese rebuilt their economy after World War II with the *Kaizen system*, which stands for "continuous betterment." They encouraged workers, at every level, to look for small and large improvements that they could make in their "line of sight."

When you practice these ideas and use them as your guide for the way you treat your coworkers, you will be amazed at how much more effective you are, and how improved your team becomes at achieving better results.

Your ability to motivate, inspire, and elicit the very best performance of the people entrusted to you will determine your success as a manager as much or more than any other factor.

Good luck!

ABOUT THE AUTHOR

Brian Tracy is a professional speaker, trainer, seminar leader, and consultant, and chairman of Brian Tracy International, a training and consulting company based in Solana Beach, California.

Brian bootstrapped his way to success. In 1981, in talks and seminars around the U.S., he began teaching the principles he forged in sales and business. Today, his books and audio and video programs—more than 500 of them—are available in 38 languages and are used in 55 countries.

He is the bestselling author of more than fifty books, including *Full Engagement* and *Reinvention.*

"Inspiring, entertaining, informative, motivational..."

Brian Tracy is one of the world's top speakers. He addresses more than 250,000 people annually—in over 100 appearances—and has consulted and trained at more than 1,000 corporations. In his career he has reached over five million people in 58 countries. He has lived and practiced every principle in his writing and speeches:

21st Century Thinking: How to out-maneuver the com - petition and get superior results in an ever-turbulent business climate.

Leadership in the New Millennium: Learn the most powerful leadership principles—ever—to get maximum results, faster.

Advanced Selling Strategies: How to use modern sales' most advanced strategies and tactics to outperform your competitors.

The Psychology of Success: Think and act like the top per-formers. Learn practical, proven techniques for excellence.

To book Brian to speak at your next meeting or conference, visit Brian Tracy International at *www.briantracy.com*, or call (858) 436-7316 for a free promotional package. Brian will carefully customize his talk to your specific needs.
